MONSTERS

21 Stories of the Most Fantastic and Gruesome Creatures of All Time—With Exercises for Developing Critical Reading Skills

Dan Dramer

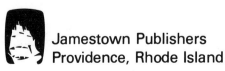 Jamestown Publishers
Providence, Rhode Island

MONSTERS
21 Stories of the Most Fantastic and Gruesome
Creatures of All Time—With Exercises for
Developing Critical Reading Skills

Catalog No. 763
Copyright ©1985 by Jamestown Publishers

Cover Illustration by Bob Eggleton
Cover and Text Design by Deborah Hulsey Christie

Printed in the United States of America

6 7 8 9 10 DP 96 95 94 93 92

ISBN 0-89061-451-2

Contents

To the Teacher   5

   Introduction

   How to Use This Book

Sample Unit   10

To the Student   16

GROUP ONE

1 The Cyclops   **18**

2 King Kong   **24**

3 Medusa   **30**

4 Bigfoot   **36**

5 Has Earth Been Visited by Creatures from UFOs?   **42**

6 The Nemean Lion and the Hound of Hell   **48**

7 Fabulous Fakes   **54**

GROUP TWO

8 Movie Monsters   **62**

9 Frankenstein's Monster   **68**

10 The Minotaur   **74**

11 Giants   **80**

12 Nessie   **86**

13 The Chimera   **92**

14 Creatures of the Imagination   **98**

GROUP THREE

15 Grendel   **106**

16 The Kraken   **112**

17 Dracula   **118**

18 The Walking Dead   **124**

19 Werewolves   **130**

20 The Yeti   **136**

21 Dragons   **142**

Answer Key   **150**

Words per Minute Table   **154**

Progress Graphs

    Reading Speed   **156**

    Critical Reading Scores   **157**

Picture Credits   **158**

To the Teacher

INTRODUCTION

Young people and adults alike have long been fascinated by monsters. The term *monster* encompasses an array of ghastly creatures from legendary and mythical entities such as the Cyclops and Count Dracula to movie space creatures with green skin and enigmas such as the Loch Ness Monster. Monsters have appeared in the folklore of peoples all over the world for thousands of years, and in literature, drama, art and movies. The grisly and the horrible seem to attract just about everyone. *Monsters* helps you to capitalize on this interest by providing stories about some of the world's most famous monsters to guide your students in the development of their critical reading skills.

Monsters provides interesting subject matter for thoughtful interpretation and exciting discussion, while challenging your students in four critical reading categories: main idea, important details, inferences, and vocabulary in context. *Monsters* can also help your students to improve their reading rates. Timing of the selections is optional, but many teachers find it an effective motivating device.

Monsters consists of twenty-one units divided into three groups of seven units each. All the stories in a group are on the same reading level. Group One is at the sixth-grade reading level, Group Two at the seventh, and Group Three at the eighth, as assessed by the Fry Formula for Estimating Readability.

HOW TO USE THIS BOOK

Introducing the Book. This text, used creatively, can be an effective tool for learning certain critical reading skills. We suggest that you begin by introducing the students to the contents and format of the book. Examine the book with the students to see how it is set up and what it is about. Discuss the students' ideas of what monsters are. Read through the table of contents as a class, to gain an overview of the topics.

The Sample Unit. To learn what is contained in each unit and how to proceed through a unit, turn to the Sample Unit on pages 10–15. After you have examined these pages yourself, work through the Sample Unit with your students, so that they may have a clear understanding of the purpose of the book and of how they are to use it.

The Sample Unit is set up exactly as the regular units are. At the beginning there is a photograph or illustration accompanied by a brief introduction to the story. The story is next, followed by four types of comprehension exercises: Finding the Main Idea, Recalling Facts, Making Inferences, and Using Words Precisely.

Begin by having someone in the class read aloud the introduction that appears with the picture. Then give the students a few moments to study the picture. Ask for their thoughts on what the story will be about. Continue the discussion for a minute or so. Then have the students read the story. (You may wish to time the students' reading, in order to help them improve their reading speed as well as their comprehension. A Words per Minute table is located in the back of the book, to help the students figure their reading rates.)

Then go through the sample questions as a class. An explanation of the comprehension skill and directions for answering the questions are given at the beginning of each exercise. Make sure all the students understand how to answer the four different types of questions and how to figure their scores. The correct answers and sample scores are printed in lighter type. Also, explanations of all the correct answers are given within the sample Main Idea and Making Inferences exercises, to help the students understand how to think through these question types.

As the students are working their way through the Sample

Unit, be sure to have them turn to the Words per Minute table on pages 154 and 155 (if you have timed their reading) and the Reading Speed and Critical Reading Scores graphs on pages 156 and 157 at the appropriate points. Explain to the students the purpose of each, and read the directions with them. Be sure they understand how the table and graphs will be used. You will probably have to help them find and mark their scores for the first unit or two.

Timing the Story. If you are going to time your students' reading, explain to them your reason for doing so: to help them keep track of and improve their reading rates.

Here's one way of timing. Have all the students in the class begin reading the story at the same time. After one minute has passed, write on the chalkboard the time that has elapsed, and begin updating it at ten-second intervals (1:00, 1:10, 1:20, etc.). Tell the students to copy down the last time shown on the chalkboard when they have finished reading. They should write their reading time in the space designated after the story.

Have the students check their reading rates by using the Words per Minute table on pages 154 and 155. They should then enter their reading speed on the Reading Speed graph on page 156. Graphing their reading rates allows the students to keep track of improvement in their reading speed.

Working Through Each Unit. If the students have carefully completed all parts of the Sample Unit, they should be ready to tackle the regular units. In each unit, begin by having someone in the class read aloud the introduction to the story, just as you did in the Sample Unit. Discuss the topic of the story, and allow the students time to study the illustration.

Then have the students read the story. If you are timing them, have the students enter their reading time, find their reading speed, and record their speed on the graph after they have finished reading the story.

Next, direct the students to complete the four comprehension exercises *without* looking back at the story. When they have finished, go over the questions and answers with them. The students will grade their own answers and make the necessary corrections. They should then enter their Critical Reading Scores on the graph on page 157.

The Graphs. Students enjoy graphing their work. Graphs show, in a concrete and easily understandable way, how a student is progressing. Seeing a line of progressively rising scores gives students the incentive to continue to strive for improvement.

Check the graphs regularly. This will allow you to establish a routine for reviewing each student's progress. Discuss with each student what the graphs show and what kind of progress you expect. Establish guidelines and warning signals so that students will know when to approach you for counseling and advice.

RELATED TEXTS

If you find that your students enjoy and benefit from the stories and skills exercises in *Monsters,* you may be interested in *Disasters!, Phenomena, Heroes, Eccentrics,* and *Apparitions:* five related Jamestown texts. All feature high-interest stories and work in four critical reading comprehension skills. As in *Monsters,* the units in those books are divided into three groups, at reading levels six, seven, and eight.

Do both good and evil exist in every human being? Is it possible that they could be separated, making one totally good person and one totally evil one?

Such thoughts often occupied the mind of Dr. Henry Jekyll. Through chance, he found the answer. It was an answer that changed his life.

The Evil Mr. Hyde

It was three o'clock in the morning in the heart of London. There were still many people about, for large cities never sleep. A dark, burly man walked quickly down a side street, paying no attention to anyone else. Coming toward him at a run was a little girl of between eight and ten years old. The two collided at the corner, and the girl fell to the ground. Then, as passersby watched in horror, the man trampled the child and left her on the ground, screaming in pain.

What sort of creature was this? Who would do such a despicable thing? It was the hideous and evil Mr. Hyde. The very sight of him caused disgust and fear in those who looked upon him.

Edward Hyde is the evil side of the good Doctor Henry Jekyll in the Robert Lewis Stevenson story *The Strange Case of Dr. Jekyll and Mr. Hyde.* Written in 1886, the novel is both a thriller and a moral tale about the good and evil sides of human nature. The basis of the story is that there are two sides to every human being. One part wants to do good and help other people. The other part delights in doing evil. Stevenson, like many others of his time, believed that the two natures are constantly at war within us. The idea is that most people succeed in hiding their bad

side. But in criminals, the evil side has won out.

In *The Strange Case of Dr. Jekyll and Mr. Hyde,* Dr. Jekyll is a good and well-respected physician. In private, he thinks a great deal about the two sides of human nature. He wonders what it would be like if the two could be separated. Wouldn't it be wonderful to have people who were totally good? Evil could then be wiped from the face of the earth!

One day, while working in his laboratory, Dr. Jekyll accidentally mixes a strange drug that has the power to separate the two personalities. He drinks the drug and instantly undergoes a strange transformation. Dreadful pains rack his body. He feels that he is being twisted inside, as though his bones are grinding. A tremendous feeling of horror comes over him. But as that feeling passes, he begins to feel lighter and younger, and also reckless and wicked! Then, upon looking into a mirror, he meets Mr. Hyde for the first time. The good and handsome doctor has been transformed into a dark, hairy, twisted, disgusting creature. He has become pure evil. Frightened, he quickly swallows another dose of the drug and is relieved to find himself restored to the personality of Dr. Jekyll.

The good doctor soon finds that he cannot control his impulse to drink the drug and transform himself. In the guise of Mr. Hyde, he goes out again and again into the city to commit horrible acts. The evil creature cares for nothing and no one. Dr. Jekyll's friends notice that Jekyll has become cold and distant. He seems to have no time for them. Meanwhile, Mr. Hyde is enjoying his freedom. He feels no guilt. Whenever he gets into some kind of trouble, he has only to run back to the laboratory and drink some of the drug. Behold! He is once again Henry Jekyll.

All this goes on for several months, until Jekyll wakes up one morning to find that during the night he has turned back into Mr. Hyde! The evil side is becoming stronger. It is becoming harder and harder to regain the body of the good doctor. Jekyll is losing hold of his better half!

Jekyll is so frightened that for a while he stops taking the drug. He does good deeds to make up for Hyde's evil acts. He spends time with his friends. But he misses Mr. Hyde. So one night he again uses the drug. The devil that has been caged for so long is stronger than ever. That night on the streets, an elderly man happens to bump into Mr. Hyde. With a gleam in his eye and delight running through his terrible being, the beast clubs the defenseless man to death with his cane. While hanging breathlessly over the dead man at his feet, Hyde suddenly becomes filled with terror. He flees from the scene and runs to the lab. A quick gulp of the drug, and he is once again Henry Jekyll. Never again, promises Jekyll. Never again.

Dr. Jekyll no longer feels the desire to become Mr. Hyde. But it is too late! Once again he begins slipping without warning into his evil side, even though he doesn't drink the drug. While sitting on a park bench, while dozing in a chair or sitting at his desk, he feels the terrible change coming over him. Looking down at his hands, he finds that they have become dark and hairy. His evil side is winning out. Finally, he is almost out of the powder with which to make the drug that enables him to return to being Dr. Jekyll. He buys more, but finds to his horror that it does not have the same effect. There was some unknown ingredient, some impurity, in the first powder that brought about the change. In disgust at the loathsome thing he is becoming, and in fear that Mr. Hyde will soon take over completely, Dr. Jekyll kills himself. In doing so, he also kills Mr. Hyde.

This story has fascinated people for more than a hundred years. More movie versions have been made of Dr. Jekyll and Mr. Hyde than of almost any other monster tale. Why are people so fascinated with this particular horror story? Perhaps it is because we can all see ourselves in it. Everyone struggles with decisions about right and wrong. Each of us sometimes chooses the attraction of what we know to be wrong or bad for us. Does evil begin to win out if you choose it too often? Is the evil within us truly as ugly and frightening as Mr. Hyde? Can we keep the monster inside us under control, or might it come to control us? ■

If you have been timed while reading this selection, enter your reading time below. Then turn to the Words per Minute table on page 154 and look up your reading speed (words per minute). When you are working through the regular units, you will then enter your reading speed on the graph on page 156.

READING TIME: Sample Unit

_____ : _____
Minutes   *Seconds*

How well did you read?

- *The four types of questions that follow appear in each unit in this book. The directions for each kind of question tell you how to mark your answers. In this Sample Unit, the answers are marked for you. Also, for the Main Idea and Making Inferences exercises, explanations of the answers are given, to help you understand how to think through these question types. Read through these exercises carefully.*

- *When you have finished all four exercises in a unit, you will check your work by using the answer key that starts on page 150. For each right answer, you will put a check mark (✓) on the line beside the box. For each wrong answer, you will write the correct answer on the line.*

- *For scoring each exercise, you will follow the directions below the questions. In this unit, sample scores are entered as examples.*

A FINDING THE MAIN IDEA

Look at the three statements below. One expresses the main idea of the story you just read. A good main idea statement answers two questions: it tells *who* or *what* is the subject of the story, and it answers the understood question *does what?* or *is what?* Another statement is *too broad*, it is vague and doesn't tell much about the topic of the story. The third statement is *too narrow*, it tells about only one part of the story.

Match the statements with the three answer choices below by writing the letter of each answer in the box in front of the statement it goes with.

M—Main Idea   **B—Too Broad**   **N—Too Narrow**

✓ [B] 1. The idea that good and evil lived side by side in human beings was a popular notion in the 1800s, and was reflected in the writings of the time.

[This statement is true, but it is *too broad*. The story is specifically about Dr. Jekyll and Mr. Hyde.]

✓ [N] 2. Mr. Hyde was a disgusting evil character in the popular Robert Louis Stevenson novel *The Strange Case of Dr. Jekyll and Mr. Hyde*.

[This statement is *too narrow*. It tells nothing about the evil side of human nature that Mr. Hyde stood for.]

✓ [M] 3. Mr. Hyde, a hideous and evil character in the novel *The Strange Case of Dr. Jekyll and Mr. Hyde*, was a symbol of the evil side of human nature.

[This statement is the *main idea*. It tells you that the reading selection is about Mr. Hyde, and it tells you the most important fact about Mr. Hyde.]

__15__ Score 15 points for a correct *M* answer
__10__ Score 5 points for each correct *B* or *N* answer
__25__ TOTAL SCORE: Finding the Main Idea

B RECALLING FACTS

How well do you remember the facts in the story you just read?
Put an *x* in the box in front of the correct answer to each of the
multiple-choice questions below.

1. The story of Dr. Jekyll and Mr. Hyde takes place in
   - ☐ a. Paris.
   - ☑ b. London.
   - ☐ c. New York.

2. Dr. Jekyll first tried to stop taking the drug when he
   - ☐ a. killed someone.
   - ☑ b. found himself turning into Mr. Hyde without taking the drug.
   - ☐ c. trampled a little girl in the streets.

3. Dr. Jekyll could no longer make the drug because
   - ☐ a. he could not buy the powder he needed.
   - ☐ b. he could no longer return to the personality of Dr. Jekyll for long enough.
   - ☑ c. the powder with which he had made it had contained some unknown ingredient.

4. Dr. Jekyll killed himself because he
   - ☑ a. had lost the ability to do away with Mr. Hyde.
   - ☐ b. was afraid he would no longer be able to escape into the personality of Mr. Hyde.
   - ☐ c. decided that people were basically evil.

5. The story of Jekyll and Hyde was written in the
   - ☐ a. 1700s.
   - ☑ b. 1800s.
   - ☐ c. 1920s.

Score 5 points for each correct answer

25 TOTAL SCORE: Recalling Facts

C MAKING INFERENCES

An inference is a judgment that is made or an idea that is
arrived at based on facts or on information that is given. You
make an inference when you understand something that is *not*
stated directly, but that is *implied*, or suggested by the facts that
are given.

Below are five statements that are judgments or ideas that
have been arrived at from the facts of the story. Write the letter
C in the box in front of each statement that is a correct inference. Write the letter *F* in front of each faulty inference.

C—Correct Inference   **F—Faulty Inference**

✓ [C] 1. Dr. Jekyll's friends did not know that he could transform himself into an evil creature.

[This is a *correct* inference. You are told that his friends noticed only that Jekyll had become distant and no longer had time for them.]

✓ [F] 2. Dr. Jekyll had always wanted to live an evil life.

[This is a *faulty* inference. You are told at the beginning that he thought it would be wonderful to be able to separate the good from the evil, and to destroy the evil.]

✓ [C] 3. At first, Dr. Jekyll found his evil side attractive and enjoyable.

[This is a *correct* inference. You are told that when Dr. Jekyll stopped taking the drug for a while he missed Hyde. He enjoyed the reckless feeling of evil.]

✓ [F] 4. Mr. Hyde had superhuman strength.

[This is a *faulty* inference. Mr. Hyde's strength is never referred to.]

✓ [F] 5. If Dr. Jekyll had been able to make more of the drug, his good side would eventually have taken over.

[This is a *faulty* inference. In the end, Mr. Hyde was taking over more and more, even though Dr. Jekyll kept taking the drug to win back his good side. Nothing indicates that that would have changed.]

Score 5 points for each correct answer

25 TOTAL SCORE: Making Inferences

D USING WORDS PRECISELY

Each of the numbered sentences below contains an underlined word or phrase from the story you have just read. Under the sentence are three definitions. One has the *same* meaning as the underlined word or phrase, one has *almost the same* meaning, and one has the *opposite* meaning. Match the definitions with the three answer choices by writing the letter that stands for each answer in the box in front of the definition it goes with.

S—Same   A—Almost the Same   O—Opposite

1. Who would do such a despicable thing?

   ✓ S a. low and mean

   ✓ A b. unfeeling

   ✓ O c. honorable

2. He quickly swallowed another dose of the drug and was relieved to find himself restored to the personality of Dr. Jekyll.

   ✓ A a. rearranged

   ✓ O b. taken away

   ✓ S c. returned

3. The good doctor soon found that he could not control his impulse to drink the drug and transform himself.

   ✓ O a. unwillingness

   ✓ S b. sudden desire

   ✓ A c. wish

4. Finally, he was almost out of the powder with which to make the drug that enabled him to return to being Dr. Jekyll.

   ✓ A a. helped

   ✓ S b. allowed

   ✓ O c. prevented

5. In disgust at the loathsome thing he was becoming, Dr. Jekyll killed himself.

   ✓ S a. disgusting

   ✓ O b. admirable

   ✓ A c. unhealthy

   15 Score 3 points for each correct *S* answer
   10 Score 1 point for each correct *A* or *O* answer
   25 TOTAL SCORE: Using Words Precisely

● *Enter the four total scores in the spaces below, and add them together to find your Critical Reading Score. Then record your Critical Reading Score on the graph on page 157.*

_____	Finding the Main Idea
_____	Recalling Facts
_____	Making Inferences
_____	Using Words Precisely
_____	CRITICAL READING SCORE: Sample Unit

To the Student

Almost everyone is fascinated by monsters. They have appeared in folklore and myths for thousands of years, and we regularly meet up with them in literature and movies. It seems that we love to be scared by the strange and terrible. *Monsters* brings you the stories of twenty-one of the world's most fascinating monsters.

While you are enjoying these intriguing stories, you will be developing your reading skills. This book assumes that you already are a fairly good reader. *Monsters* is for students who want to read faster and to increase their understanding of what they read. If you complete all twenty-one units—reading the stories and completing the exercises—you will surely improve both your reading rate and your comprehension.

GROUP ONE

The Cyclops

It was almost three thousand years ago that the Greek epic poet Homer wrote his great tale of adventure, *The Odyssey*. His hero is Ulysses, king of Ithaca. After fighting for Greece in the Trojan War, Ulysses and his men are trying to return home. They meet many obstacles along the way.

At one point in their journey, the Greek warriors came upon an unknown island in the Aegean Sea. When he saw the island, Ulysses decided to stop and explore. His ships were running low on supplies, and Ulysses hoped he could stock up with provisions from the island. Besides, his men were tired. They had just finished fighting a war against the Trojans and were in need of a rest. Also, being a great adventurer, Ulysses wanted to see what kind of people lived on the island.

The ships anchored in the harbor of the island, and most of the men stayed on board to relax. Ulysses took twelve crew members and went ashore. They carried jugs of a very special wine as gifts for the natives.

In those days, it was the custom for people to show hospitality to travelers. Ulysses, therefore, expected a warm welcome from the inhabitants of the island. What he did not know, however, was that this land was the home of the Cyclopes (seye-CLO-peez). The Cyclopes were a race

of giants who were primitive and cruel. In the ancient Greek language, *cyclops* meant "round eye." And indeed, each giant on the island had just one round eye, right in the middle of his forehead. The Cyclopes lived on plants that grew wild on their island. They raised giant goats and sheep that provided them with milk and cheese. And contrary to what Ulysses expected, the Cyclopes did not welcome visitors. In fact, they thought nothing of killing any strangers who ventured onto their island.

Because Ulysses did not know the manner of people he was about to encounter, he and his twelve companions roamed the island freely. They did not run into any Cyclopes, but they did stumble upon one of the giants' homes. It was a huge cave dug in the side of a hill. When Ulysses and his men entered it, they found gigantic pails, bowls of milk, and plates of cheese. The men were still marveling at the size of these things when they heard a noise at the mouth of the cave.

Turning quickly, they saw a dirty, shaggy mountain of a man standing in the entrance. It was the Cyclops Polyphemus (PAHL-uh-FEE-mus), the giant who lived there. The brute was clothed in the greasy skins of sheep, and the eye in the center of his forehead was bulging. He was holding

an immense bundle of firewood, which he dropped near the mouth of the cave. Then he began to drive his giant sheep into the cave. He was so busy with his work that he didn't notice the Greeks who huddled in silence near the back of the cave. When Polyphemus had herded all his animals into the cave, he too stepped inside. Then he rolled an enormous stone across the entrance, trapping the sheep in the cave for the night. Although he did not realize it, his barricade trapped Ulysses and his twelve companions, as well.

The Greeks hiding in the shadows could only hope that the Cyclops would not spot them. After the giant had milked his ewes, however, he lit a fire, and in the light he immediately caught sight of the Greeks. In a great growling voice, he demanded to know the identity of these men who had dared to come, uninvited, into his home. Ulysses answered the Cyclops most politely. He explained that he and his men were Greeks on their way home from battle. In the name of the gods, he asked for the hospitality granted every traveler.

Polyphemus did not respond to Ulysses' request. Instead, he grabbed up two of the Greeks and hurled them against the floor of the cave, shattering them. As Ulysses and the ten remaining men watched in horror, Polyphemus devoured the broken bodies of their comrades. He followed his gory meal with a long drink of milk, then stretched out on the floor and fell fast asleep.

Ulysses' first impulse was to run his sword through the body of the sleeping giant, but he fought back the temptation. He realized that if he killed the Cyclops now, he would never be able to get out of the cave. The rock that blocked the entrance was much too heavy for Ulysses and his men to move. For the moment, at least, there was nothing Ulysses could do.

The next morning, Polyphemus killed and ate two more of the Greeks. Again Ulysses and the others were helpless to stop him. After his feast of human flesh, the Cyclops moved the rock and herded his sheep out of the cave. Then, from outside, he rolled the rock back into place.

With the Cyclops out of the cave for the day, Ulysses and his companions went to work. Ulysses had thought of a plan for escape. On the floor of the cave was a large tree trunk. Polyphemus had brought it in to make a walking stick, but Ulysses had other ideas. The Greeks cut off a section of the trunk, and all that day they worked with their swords to sharpen one end to a point.

That night when Polyphemus returned to the cave with his flock, the tree trunk

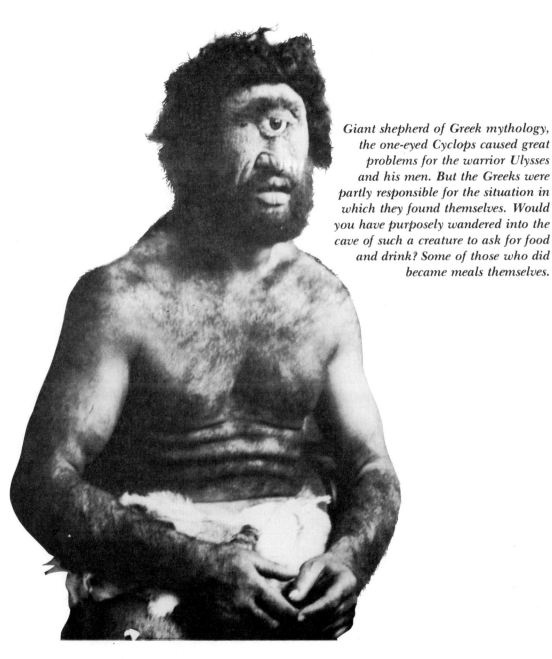

Giant shepherd of Greek mythology, the one-eyed Cyclops caused great problems for the warrior Ulysses and his men. But the Greeks were partly responsible for the situation in which they found themselves. Would you have purposely wandered into the cave of such a creature to ask for food and drink? Some of those who did became meals themselves.

was out of sight. Polyphemus lit a fire, and then he saw Ulysses coming forward with a jug of wine. Ulysses offered the wine to the Cyclops, explaining that it was a gift. Polyphemus drank from the jug and was delighted with the wine. "Tell me your name," said Polyphemus, "so that I may know who has given me this wonderful present." The wily Ulysses did not want to tell Polyphemus his real name, so he answered, "Nobody is my name. Nobody is what my parents named me."

"Well, Nobody, I have a gift for you too," Polyphemus said. "I shall save you until the end. You will be the last Greek I eat!" After saying those words, the Cyclops scooped up two more of Ulysses' crew members. The giant watched them squirm like puppies in his huge fist, then he popped them into his mouth and ate them. Next he drank down the wine that Ulysses had offered him. He soon fell sound asleep.

As the Cyclops lay unconscious on the stone floor, Ulysses seized the tree trunk by its dull end. With his men helping him, he plunged the sharpened end into the fire. When the point glowed red, Ulysses and his men drove the glowing point into the sleeping giant's eye. Before the startled

Cyclops could pull the blazing tree trunk from his eye, the Greeks spun it around the eye socket several times. When Polyphemus finally pulled it loose, he was completely blinded. He bellowed in pain.

Other Cyclopes in nearby caves heard Polyphemus screaming. They called out to him, "Who is hurting you? You yell as if somebody is killing you."

"Nobody is hurting me. Nobody is killing me!" cried Polyphemus.

The other Cyclopes called back, "If nobody is hurting you and nobody is killing you, there is no way we can help." With that, the other Cyclopes went back to sleep.

When morning came, the giant sheep were eager to leave the cave for their pasture. Polyphemus rolled the stone from the mouth of the cave. But then he sat down in the entrance, his arms and legs spread wide. He would let out his flock, but he was not going to let the Greeks get away.

Ulysses had anticipated that move. He had a plan for getting by the giant. Taking some rope, he tied the sheep together, side-by-side, in groups of three. Then he instructed his men to each cling to the belly of a sheep in the middle of a trio. Ulysses himself hung under the belly

of the largest sheep, which was not attached to any others. As the groups of sheep headed out of the cave, the blinded Cyclops felt each one. When he felt nothing but their woolly backs, he let them pass. He was convinced that the Greeks were still hiding in the cave.

As soon as Ulysses and his men were safely out of the cave, they let go of the sheep and ran for their ship. When they arrived, the crew on board was overjoyed. The men on the ships had almost given up hope of seeing their leader or their friends again. Ulysses quickly gave the command to sail, and the Greeks headed for home. ■

If you have been timed while reading this selection, enter your reading time below. Then turn to the Words per Minute table on page 154 and look up your reading speed (words per minute). Enter your reading speed on the graph on page 156.

READING TIME: Unit 1

_____ : _____
Minutes   *Seconds*

How well did you read?

- *Answer the four types of questions that follow. The directions for each type of question tell you how to mark your answers.*

- *When you have finished all four exercises, check your work by using the answer key on page 150. For each right answer, put a check mark (✔) on the line beside the box. For each wrong answer, write the correct answer on the line.*

- *For scoring each exercise, follow the directions below the questions.*

A FINDING THE MAIN IDEA

Look at the three statements below. One expresses the main idea of the story you just read. A good main idea statement answers two questions: it tells *who* or *what* is the subject of the story, and it answers the understood question *does what?* or *is what?* Another statement is *too broad*, it is vague and doesn't tell much about the topic of the story. The third statement is *too narrow*, it tells about only one part of the story.

Match the statements with the three answer choices below by writing the letter of each answer in the box in front of the statement it goes with.

M—Main Idea   **B—Too Broad**   **N—Too Narrow**

____ ☐ 1. The Cyclops trapped Ulysses and his twelve companions and began eating them, but Ulysses finally outsmarted the giant and escaped with six of his men.

____ ☐ 2. Ulysses and twelve of his men met with great danger on the island of the Cyclopes.

____ ☐ 3. Ulysses and his men drove a burning spike into the eye of the Cyclops Polyphemus and blinded him.

____ Score 15 points for a correct *M* answer

____ Score 5 points for each correct *B* or *N* answer

____ TOTAL SCORE: Finding the Main Idea

B RECALLING FACTS

How well do you remember the facts in the story you just read? Put an x in the box in front of the correct answer to each of the multiple-choice questions below.

1. The Cyclops herded
____ ☐ a. cows.
____ ☐ b. wild pigs.
____ ☐ c. goats and sheep.

2. How many Greeks did Polyphemus eat?
____ ☐ a. Twelve
____ ☐ b. Six
____ ☐ c. Four

3. What did Ulysses give to Polyphemus?
____ ☐ a. Wine
____ ☐ b. Cheese
____ ☐ c. Milk

4. Polyphemus's gift to Ulysses was
____ ☐ a. a promise to kill him last.
____ ☐ b. a greasy sheepskin.
____ ☐ c. some wine.

5. Ulysses and his men escaped by
____ ☐ a. riding on the backs of sheep.
____ ☐ b. covering themselves with sheepskins.
____ ☐ c. riding on the bellies of sheep.

Score 5 points for each correct answer

____ TOTAL SCORE: Recalling Facts

C MAKING INFERENCES

An inference is a judgment that is made or an idea that is arrived at based on facts or on information that is given. You make an inference when you understand something that is *not* stated directly, but that is *implied*, or suggested by the facts that are given.

Below are five statements that are judgments or ideas that have been arrived at from the facts of the story. Write the letter *C* in the box in front of each statement that is a correct inference. Write the letter *F* in front of each faulty inference.

C—Correct Inference   **F—Faulty Inference**

____ ☐ 1. Ulysses had no fear of the Cyclops.

____ ☐ 2. The other Cyclopes would have helped Polyphemus when he was being attacked by the Greeks if they had understood that "Nobody" was a person.

____ ☐ 3. Polyphemus was very smart as well as very strong.

____ ☐ 4. Ulysses' plan would not have worked if Polyphemus had had two eyes.

____ ☐ 5. Ulysses gave Polyphemus the wine in order to get him drunk and sleepy.

Score 5 points for each correct answer

____ TOTAL SCORE: Making Inferences

D USING WORDS PRECISELY

Each of the numbered sentences below contains an underlined word or phrase from the story you have just read. Under the sentence are three definitions. One has the *same* meaning as the underlined word or phrase, one has *almost the same* meaning, and one has the *opposite* meaning. Match the definitions with the three answer choices by writing the letter that stands for each answer in the box in front of the definition it goes with.

S—Same   A—Almost the Same   O—Opposite

1. Ulysses, therefore, expected a warm welcome from the <u>inhabitants</u> of the island.

____ ☐ a. residents

____ ☐ b. settlers

____ ☐ c. visitors

2. And <u>contrary</u> to what Ulysses expected, the Cyclopes did not welcome visitors.

____ ☐ a. against

____ ☐ b. just the same

____ ☐ c. opposite

3. Because Ulysses did not know the manner of people he was about to <u>encounter</u>, he and his twelve companions roamed the island freely.

____ ☐ a. look upon

____ ☐ b. meet

____ ☐ c. avoid

4. He followed his <u>gory</u> meal with a long drink of milk, then stretched out on the floor and fell fast asleep.

____ ☐ a. clean, pure

____ ☐ b. messy

____ ☐ c. bloody

5. Ulysses had <u>anticipated</u> that move. He had a plan for getting by the giant.

____ ☐ a. expected

____ ☐ b. thought of

____ ☐ c. been unprepared for

____ Score 3 points for each correct *S* answer

____ Score 1 point for each correct *A* or *O* answer

____ TOTAL SCORE: Using Words Precisely

● *Enter the four total scores in the spaces below, and add them together to find your Critical Reading Score. Then record your Critical Reading Score on the graph on page 157.*

_____ Finding the Main Idea
_____ Recalling Facts
_____ Making Inferences
_____ Using Words Precisely

_____ CRITICAL READING SCORE: Unit 1

King Kong

The gigantic ape stands atop the Empire State Building in the middle of New York City. In his hand he holds a beautiful woman. Moving gently, he places the woman on a window ledge, the safest spot he can find. Then he turns to bravely face the approaching airplanes. He knows the pilots of the planes are out to kill him, but he will not surrender. After all, he is Kong—King Kong, the most powerful creature ever born.

When Kong was living on his own tropical island, he truly was a king. He ruled over every creature in the jungle. Then humans landed on the island. When they discovered the huge ape, they saw not a proud and magnificent creature, but a chance for fame and fortune. They placed Kong in chains and took him to New York, where he was put on public display. People stared at and mocked him.

Now Kong has broken free from his bonds. He has taken the woman he loves and has climbed to the top of the tallest building in the world, hoping to escape from the men who are trying to recapture him. But as the airplanes move in, Kong sees that there is no escape. The only thing he can do is hold his ground and fight back.

When the planes begin their attack, Kong raises one of his giant arms and tries to swat them away. But they move too quickly. Their guns spray a shower of bullets at Kong and then the planes zoom out of his reach. From the sidewalk below, the people of New York watch as the bullets tear into the gorilla's enormous furry body. Again and again the planes swoop in and fire their deadly bursts. Each time, they are able to fly away before Kong can grab them. He swings his arms frantically, trying desperately to fend off his attackers. But when the movie camera zooms in for a close-up, we see that hundreds of bullets have already pierced the ape's thick hide. Blood pours from wounds all over his body. It appears that the great Kong has lost the battle.

But then, in one swift movement, Kong manages to reach out and grab a plane. As his giant fist closes around it, we hear the crunch of glass and metal. Although we know that there is a pilot trapped inside the airplane, we do not care. We are too caught up in Kong's struggle for survival. We find ourselves rooting for him to destroy the men who are his enemies. When he crushes the airplane and defiantly flings it away, we cheer. For a moment we feel that Kong is once again king.

But his triumph is all too brief. Not even the mighty Kong can withstand the power of modern weapons. As more and more bullets tear into his body, the great beast weakens and sways. His blood seeps out from the gashes in his body. Finally, Kong topples to the pavement far below with a tremendous, earth-shattering thud. Kong's great heart continues to beat for just one more moment, before becoming forever still.

So ends the story of King Kong. The movie that portrays the story of King Kong leaves the audience mourning for the fallen ape. And that is exactly what the creator of the movie wanted. His name was Merian C. Cooper. Cooper got the idea for the King Kong movie in 1929 when he was in Africa. He was there to photograph animals for another film. During his stay, however, he became interested in gorillas. He decided to make a movie about a giant ape with superior intelligence running amok on the streets of a big city.

Cooper initially intended to film the movie in Africa. But a friend in the movie industry introduced him to a man named Willis O'Brien, who had built many animal models and jungle landscapes for movies. When Cooper saw O'Brien's work, he was greatly impressed. He was so impressed, in fact, that he decided to film *King Kong* in a studio, using O'Brien's models and landscapes.

Work on the picture began in 1932. Because it required the use of numerous special effects, it was a difficult and time-consuming movie to make. Cooper had to animate the models of Kong and the other jungle animals. He also had to find a way to animate doll-sized figures of humans that were used in place of actors in some of the scenes. The dolls were used with the Kong model, which was about the size of a person, to make the ape appear gigantic in comparison to humans. In some scenes, for instance, Kong grabbed the tiny "people" in what appeared to be a huge paw. The people models were sixteen inches tall and made of rubber and sponge. Kong's shaggy body was a covering of dyed lambskin. The core of each model was a jointed metal frame. The joints allowed the model to be set in different positions.

Action was photographed by shooting a single frame, then moving the joints slightly and taking another picture, and so on. Sometimes a model was moved as little as a quarter of an inch for each shot. It took dozens of such move-and-shoot pictures just to complete a single movement such as the swinging of an arm or the taking of a step. Although the models were finely detailed, Cooper felt they weren't quite realistic enough for

Standing atop the Empire State Building, the mighty Kong raged against those who were trying to kill him. Against hopeless odds, he fought for his life. And he fought for the beautiful woman he loved. Could a gorilla be a hero? King Kong was. The big ape became one of the best-loved monsters of all time.

close shots. So for close-ups he used a huge model of Kong's head and hand, with real actors.

It took one year and $650,000 to make *King Kong*. At that time, that was a tremendous amount of money to spend on a film. Most of the money went for special effects, and the investment paid off. When the move-and-shoot pictures were projected on the screen, they looked amazingly lifelike. The close-ups of Kong's head and hand looked so real they were frightening. As word of the movie spread, audiences flocked to movie theaters to see it. The film was so successful that other producers decided to cash in on the theme of sympathetic apes. Eventually there was a whole series of films about giant apes. Among them were *Son of Kong* (1933), *Mighty Joe Young* (1949), *King Kong versus Godzilla* (1962), and *King Kong Escapes* (1967).

In 1976, when the original *King Kong* was forty-three years old, a new version of the picture was made. The story remained essentially unchanged. The new *King Kong* simply brought the old film up to date. In 1976 the Empire State Building was no longer the tallest building in the world—the twin towers of Manhattan's World Trade Center were taller. So the new film had Kong climb one of those towers. The remake also replaced the little biplanes that buzzed around Kong with helicopter gunships. The World War I machine guns of the first film became twenty-millimeter cannons whose revolving barrels spit thousands of bullets per second.

The modern weapons rip bigger, bloodier holes in Kong, but the effect on both ape and audience remains the same. Kong still fights heroically against the deadly weapons of humans. The audience cheers when Kong grabs and destroys a helicopter that ventures too close to his great arms. And of course, in the end, the great Kong collapses and dies.

A lot of people who are familiar with the original *King Kong* are disappointed that the new version does not end with the same words as the original. In the first film, as Kong lies dead on the pavement, reporters gather around his body. Carl Denham, the man who captured Kong in the jungle and brought him to New York, also stands over the body. Denham knows that it was Kong's love for the beautiful woman that led to his capture and, ultimately, to his death. So as he gazes at Kong's pitiful remains, Denham says, "That's your story, boys. It was Beauty killed the Beast."

In many ways, that's what *King Kong* is—the story of Beauty and the Beast. It is the idea of the beast falling hopelessly in love with the beauty that makes our hearts go out to poor Kong. In the classic story of *Beauty and the Beast*, the hideous beast that loves the beautiful girl turns into a handsome prince in the end. The two then go off together to live happily ever after. In *King Kong*, too, the beautiful woman goes off with a handsome man to live happily ever after. But the man is someone who helped to rescue the woman from the great ape. The poor Beast lives on only in the memories of movie fans. ∎

If you have been timed while reading this selection, enter your reading time below. Then turn to the Words per Minute table on page 154 and look up your reading speed (words per minute). Enter your reading speed on the graph on page 156.

READING TIME: Unit 2

_____ : _____
Minutes   *Seconds*

How well did you read?

- *Answer the four types of questions that follow. The directions for each type of question tell you how to mark your answers.*

- *When you have finished all four exercises, check your work by using the answer key on page 150. For each right answer, put a check mark (✔) on the line beside the box. For each wrong answer, write the correct answer on the line.*

- *For scoring each exercise, follow the directions below the questions.*

A FINDING THE MAIN IDEA

Look at the three statements below. One expresses the main idea of the story you just read. A good main idea statement answers two questions: it tells *who* or *what* is the subject of the story, and it answers the understood question *does what?* or *is what?* Another statement is *too broad*, it is vague and doesn't tell much about the topic of the story. The third statement is *too narrow*, it tells about only one part of the story.

Match the statements with the three answer choices below by writing the letter of each answer in the box in front of the statement it goes with.

M—Main Idea　　**B—Too Broad**　　**N—Too Narrow**

_____ ☐ 1. *King Kong*, whose story is patterned after the classic story of Beauty and the Beast, is one of the most successful monster movies of all time.

_____ ☐ 2. A remake of *King Kong* in 1976 stuck very close to the original version made in 1933.

_____ ☐ 3. *King Kong* has continued to capture people's hearts and imaginations for over fifty years.

_____ Score 15 points for a correct *M* answer
_____ Score 5 points for each correct *B* or *N* answer

_____ TOTAL SCORE: Finding the Main Idea

B RECALLING FACTS

How well do you remember the facts in the story you just read? Put an *x* in the box in front of the correct answer to each of the multiple-choice questions below.

1. In the story, King Kong is captured from his home
   - ____ ☐ a. in Polynesia.
   - ____ ☐ b. in Africa.
   - ____ ☐ c. on an island.

2. Merian Cooper got the inspiration for King Kong while he was in
   - ____ ☐ a. Willis O'Brien's studio.
   - ____ ☐ b. Africa.
   - ____ ☐ c. a zoo.

3. The figure of King Kong was
   - ____ ☐ a. a trained gorilla.
   - ____ ☐ b. an animated model of a gorilla.
   - ____ ☐ c. a person in a gorilla costume.

4. In the remake of the movie, King Kong fights his final battle from atop the
   - ____ ☐ a. Sears Tower.
   - ____ ☐ b. World Trade Center.
   - ____ ☐ c. Empire State Building.

5. The 1976 film differed from the original in
   - ____ ☐ a. the last words that were spoken.
   - ____ ☐ b. the way in which Kong met his death.
   - ____ ☐ c. the audience's reaction to the movie.

Score 5 points for each correct answer

____ TOTAL SCORE: Recalling Facts

C MAKING INFERENCES

An inference is a judgment that is made or an idea that is arrived at based on facts or on information that is given. You make an inference when you understand something that is *not* stated directly, but that is *implied*, or suggested by the facts that are given.

Below are five statements that are judgments or ideas that have been arrived at from the facts of the story. Write the letter *C* in the box in front of each statement that is a correct inference. Write the letter *F* in front of each faulty inference.

C—Correct Inference   F—Faulty Inference

- ____ ☐ 1. People continue to like *King Kong* because its story is one that people of all times and places can relate to.

- ____ ☐ 2. The ape movies that followed *King Kong* were all tremendously successful.

- ____ ☐ 3. *King Kong* made a lot of money for the studio that produced it.

- ____ ☐ 4. The special effects used in the original *King Kong* were as convincing as any modern effects could be.

- ____ ☐ 5. *King Kong* is the most successful monster movie ever made.

Score 5 points for each correct answer

____ TOTAL SCORE: Making Inferences

D USING WORDS PRECISELY

Each of the numbered sentences below contains an underlined word or phrase from the story you have just read. Under the sentence are three definitions. One has the *same* meaning as the underlined word or phrase, one has *almost the same* meaning, and one has the *opposite* meaning. Match the definitions with the three answer choices by writing the letter that stands for each answer in the box in front of the definition it goes with.

S—Same   A—Almost the Same   O—Opposite

1. But when the movie camera zooms in for a close-up, we see that hundreds of bullets have already <u>pierced</u> the ape's thick hide.

   ____ ☐ a. healed

   ____ ☐ b. opened

   ____ ☐ c. torn into

2. Cooper <u>initially</u> intended to film the movie in Africa.

   ____ ☐ a. originally

   ____ ☐ b. in the end

   ____ ☐ c. before

3. The audience cheers when Kong grabs and destroys a helicopter that <u>ventures</u> too close to his great arms.

   ____ ☐ a. avoids approaching

   ____ ☐ b. strays

   ____ ☐ c. dares to go

4. Not even the mighty Kong can <u>withstand</u> the power of modern weapons.

   ____ ☐ a. face

   ____ ☐ b. hold out against

   ____ ☐ c. give in to

5. Denham knows that it was Kong's love for the beautiful woman that led to his capture and, <u>ultimately</u>, to his death.

   ____ ☐ a. finally

   ____ ☐ b. originally

   ____ ☐ c. afterwards

____ Score 3 points for each correct S answer

____ Score 1 point for each correct A or O answer

____ TOTAL SCORE: Using Words Precisely

- *Enter the four total scores in the spaces below, and add them together to find your Critical Reading Score. Then record your Critical Reading Score on the graph on page 157.*

_____	Finding the Main Idea
_____	Recalling Facts
_____	Making Inferences
_____	Using Words Precisely
_____	CRITICAL READING SCORE: Unit 2

Medusa's face held so much evil that no one who looked upon it could live. Yet Perseus was sent to destroy the monster. Could he succeed in such a task? Not alone, perhaps. But Perseus had the gods on his side.

Medusa

The king's lips curled up into a cruel smile. King Polydectes, a mythical ruler in ancient Greece, was intensely pleased with himself. For a long time he had been trying to think of a way to kill a young man named Perseus. The king wanted to marry Perseus's beautiful mother, but he was afraid Perseus would stand in his way. Now, at last, he thought he had found a way to get rid of Perseus. He was confident that he had planned the perfect crime.

The king's plan was to ask Perseus to go on a mission to prove his courage and manliness. The mission would be to seek out and kill a monster named Medusa. Many men had tried to kill Medusa, but all had been destroyed by her. The king was sure that Perseus, too, would lose his life to the monster. The plan was perfect because Perseus would die but no one would accuse the king of being a murderer. Everyone would simply think that Perseus had gotten himself killed while trying to be a hero.

The wicked king summoned Perseus to his castle and pretended to be friendly. He put his arm around the young man's shoulders. "Perseus," he said, "at some point, all men must find a way to prove their courage. I have a challenge for you that will allow you to do this. Your challenge is to slay Medusa and bring me her head. Her head will be proof to everyone of your bravery."

When Perseus heard the king's challenge, he was frightened. He knew all about Medusa. She was the fiercest of all monsters. Once she had been a beautiful maiden. But she had angered the gods. In their wrath, they had turned her into a hideous monster. Now she had long, curved claws, powerful wings and sharp fangs. For hair, she had a mass of hissing, snarling snakes that were constantly coiling and striking. But deadliest of all was her face. It was so full of evil that anyone who looked at it was instantly turned to stone. Although Perseus was nervous as he contemplated all this, he did not want to seem like a coward. He said bravely, "I will bring you Medusa's head." The king was delighted. His plan was working.

As Perseus set out on his mission, there was little chance that he would succeed. Luckily, Zeus, king of the gods, was aware of the king's scheme. Zeus called on the other gods to help Perseus. Hermes, swiftest of the gods, gave Perseus a pair of wings for his feet, so that he could travel quickly. The goddess Athena gave him a shield with a mirrorlike surface. "When you reach Medusa," Athena explained, "look only at her reflection in the shield. If you gaze directly at her, you will be turned to stone."

Armed with the wings and the shield, Perseus quickly made his way to the land where Medusa lived. Along the last few miles, he saw many men who had been turned to stone. They stood frozen in place for all time. When at last he reached the hollow where the monster lived, Perseus saw that the ground was covered with petrified figures. Quickly he turned his back and, using his mirrored shield to guide him, began walking backward toward the hollow.

As Perseus neared the center of the hollow, he saw something moving in the reflection from his shield. It was the snakes on Medusa's head, shimmering in the mirror. The serpents seemed relatively peaceful. Perseus guessed that Medusa was asleep. He hoped to slay her while she slept, but as he edged closer his foot accidently kicked a stone. The stone clattered down into the hollow, and the monster awoke. Her mighty roar filled the air. Looking into his shield, Perseus could see her rise into view, her jaws agape and her terrible eyes flashing. The snakes on her head writhed and coiled.

With his back still turned, Perseus drew his sword. The creature hesitated for a moment, as if surprised that this man was not turning to stone. Then, snake heads hissing, Medusa rushed toward Perseus.

Perseus's heart pounded as the monster approached. He stood with his legs spread wide, braced for action. With one hand he held up his shield. In the other he gripped his sword. Soon Medusa was so close that Perseus could feel her hot breath on his neck. Still he stood his ground. He waited until her mouth was about to clamp down on him. Then he swept his sword around behind him in a slashing blow. He felt the cutting edge bite into Medusa's neck. There was a terrible cry. Then there was silence.

Perseus surveyed the dead monster's reflection. He did not turn to look at it with his own eyes. The gods had warned him that even in death Medusa's face would turn a person to stone. Carefully Perseus reached behind him and picked up the snake-covered head. He dropped it into a sack and began his return journey.

When Perseus arrived home, he found his mother in tears. She had been forced to agree to a marriage with King Polydectes. Perseus was furious. He went straight to the king's castle to confront him. When the king saw the young man, he was shocked. He had been sure that Perseus would not return. As Polydectes watched, Perseus turned his head away and reached into his sack. Seeing that Perseus wasn't looking, the king grabbed a sword. Before he could strike, however, Perseus pulled the head of Medusa from the sack, and the king was instantly turned to stone.

Perseus became a hero in his kingdom. He had saved his mother from a marriage to a tyrant. He had freed the people from the rule of the evil Polydectes. And he had killed the fierce Medusa. ■

If you have been timed while reading this selection, enter your reading time below. Then turn to the Words per Minute table on page 154 and look up your reading speed (words per minute). Enter your reading speed on the graph on page 156.

READING TIME: Unit 3

_____ : _____
Minutes   *Seconds*

How well did you read?

- *Answer the four types of questions that follow. The directions for each type of question tell you how to mark your answers.*

- *When you have finished all four exercises, check your work by using the answer key on page 150. For each right answer, put a check mark (✔) on the line beside the box. For each wrong answer, write the correct answer on the line.*

- *For scoring each exercise, follow the directions below the questions.*

A   FINDING THE MAIN IDEA

Look at the three statements below. One expresses the main idea of the story you just read. A good main idea statement answers two questions: it tells *who* or *what* is the subject of the story, and it answers the understood question *does what?* or *is what?* Another statement is *too broad*, it is vague and doesn't tell much about the topic of the story. The third statement is *too narrow*, it tells about only one part of the story.

Match the statements with the three answer choices below by writing the letter of each answer in the box in front of the statement it goes with.

M—Main Idea   B—Too Broad   N—Too Narrow

_____ ☐ 1. Perseus, with the help of the gods, killed Medusa and saved his mother from the evil king Polydectes.

_____ ☐ 2. The evil king Polydectes tried to do away with Perseus by having him go after the terrible Medusa.

_____ ☐ 3. Perseus and the monster Medusa met in a fight to the death.

_____ Score 15 points for a correct *M* answer
_____ Score 5 points for each correct *B* or *N* answer

_____ TOTAL SCORE: Finding the Main Idea

B RECALLING FACTS

How well do you remember the facts in the story you just read?
Put an x in the box in front of the correct answer to each of the
multiple-choice questions below.

1. Polydectes told Perseus that slaying the monster
   would
   - ☐ a. prevent the king's marriage to Perseus's mother.
   - ☐ b. rid the kingdom of an evil force.
   - ☐ c. prove Perseus's courage and manliness.

2. The hollow where Medusa lived was surrounded by
   - ☐ a. stone figures of men.
   - ☐ b. snakes.
   - ☐ c. Greek gods.

3. Medusa was awakened by
   - ☐ a. the writhing of the snakes on her head.
   - ☐ b. a clattering stone.
   - ☐ c. the reflection from Perseus's shiny shield.

4. When Perseus beheaded Medusa, she was
   - ☐ a. above him.
   - ☐ b. behind him.
   - ☐ c. below him.

5. Perseus arrived home to find his mother
   - ☐ a. married to Polydectes.
   - ☐ b. dead of a broken heart.
   - ☐ c. about to marry Polydectes.

Score 5 points for each correct answer

___ TOTAL SCORE: Recalling Facts

C MAKING INFERENCES

An inference is a judgment that is made or an idea that is
arrived at based on facts or on information that is given. You
make an inference when you understand something that is *not*
stated directly, but that is *implied*, or suggested by the facts that
are given.

Below are five statements that are judgments or ideas that
have been arrived at from the facts of the story. Write the letter
C in the box in front of each statement that is a correct inference. Write the letter F in front of each faulty inference.

C—Correct Inference   F—Faulty Inference

- ☐ 1. Perseus was a god.

- ☐ 2. When Perseus set out to slay Medusa, he did not
   know that Polydectes wanted to marry his mother.

- ☐ 3. Without the help of the gods, Perseus could not
   have killed Medusa.

- ☐ 4. Medusa had no fear of any human.

- ☐ 5. When Perseus had killed the Medusa, all those
   who had been turned to stone came back to life.

Score 5 points for each correct answer

___ TOTAL SCORE: Making Inferences

D USING WORDS PRECISELY

Each of the numbered sentences below contains an underlined word or phrase from the story you have just read. Under the sentence are three definitions. One has the *same* meaning as the underlined word or phrase, one has *almost the same* meaning, and one has the *opposite* meaning. Match the definitions with the three answer choices by writing the letter that stands for each answer in the box in front of the definition it goes with.

S—Same   A—Almost the Same   O—Opposite

1. He was <u>confident</u> that he had planned the perfect crime.

___ ☐ a. determined

___ ☐ b. sure

___ ☐ c. uncertain

2. Although Perseus was nervous as he <u>contemplated</u> all of this, he did not want to seem like a coward.

___ ☐ a. thought about

___ ☐ b. ignored

___ ☐ c. studied

3. King Polydectes, a mythical ruler in ancient Greece, was <u>intensely</u> pleased with himself.

___ ☐ a. slightly

___ ☐ b. strongly

___ ☐ c. very

4. Looking into his shield, Perseus could see her rise into view, her jaws <u>agape</u> and her terrible eyes flashing.

___ ☐ a. wide open

___ ☐ b. parted

___ ☐ c. shut tight

5. In their <u>wrath</u>, they had turned her into a hideous monster.

___ ☐ a. irritation

___ ☐ b. anger

___ ☐ c. calmness

___ Score 3 points for each correct *S* answer

___ Score 1 point for each correct *A* or *O* answer

___ TOTAL SCORE: Using Words Precisely

● *Enter the four total scores in the spaces below, and add them together to find your Critical Reading Score. Then record your Critical Reading Score on the graph on page 157.*

___ Finding the Main Idea
___ Recalling Facts
___ Making Inferences
___ Using Words Precisely
___ CRITICAL READING SCORE: Unit 3

In 1967, in a thickly forested area of northern California, monster buffs Roger Patterson and Bob Gimlin went looking for Bigfoot. They had a movie camera with them, just in case they got lucky. The fuzzy photograph shown here is from some film they shot of a seven-foot-tall apelike creature they claim they saw on that expedition. Is it possible that huge beasts that are half human and half ape live in the wilderness areas of North America's Pacific Coast? Or are people in ape suits and giant fake feet trying to pull off a Bighoax?

Bigfoot

He is known as Bigfoot. For years his very name has struck terror into the hearts of people on the Pacific Coast of North America. Hundreds claim to have seen him. Some know him by other names, such as Sasquatch, MoMo or Skunk Ape. But all agree on what he looks like. He is reported to be between seven and nine feet tall, with large red eyes that glow in the dark. A sickening odor emanates from his hairy body. He has huge feet that make footprints measuring over fifteen inches long.

Stories of Bigfoot have been around since the days of the early American Indians. Old Indian tales tell of wild men that were part animal. They were huge and hairy, with glowing eyes. According to the legends, they not only killed and ate cattle, but also ate human beings.

There have been equally gruesome stories of Bigfoot in more recent times. One such story involves four gold miners. They built a cabin in a canyon near the volcano Mount St. Helens in Washington State. In 1924, they moved into the cabin and lived there peacefully until someone— or something—began to rob their camp. When the miners looked for signs of the intruder, they discovered huge footprints in the dirt. Worried, the men began carrying guns.

One day soon after, the miners spied two apelike animals at the edge of a nearby cliff. Quickly the men raised their rifles and began shooting at the beasts. The bullets appeared to wound one animal, but it ran away. The second animal seemed to have been killed. All four men saw it plunge over the precipice. When they went to look for the body, however, they found nothing.

That night the men were awakened by a heavy pounding on the cabin roof and walls. Someone was throwing rocks at their cabin! The miners didn't dare go outside. They just stuck their rifles through cracks in the cabin walls and began firing. It was too dark to aim, but the men felt that they had to do something to protect themselves. When dawn arrived, the bombardment of rocks stopped. The miners stepped out and looked around. They saw rocks, blood and enormous footprints all around the cabin.

It didn't take long for the miners' story to spread. As more and more people heard of the "apes" that had attacked the four men, the canyon became known as Ape Valley. It is still known by that name.

The four gold miners were not the only ones to run into Bigfoot in 1924. A prospector working near Vancouver, British Columbia, also claimed to see the creature that season. In fact, he claimed that he was kidnapped by a Bigfoot. The man said that he had been asleep in his sleeping bag when a Bigfoot appeared. The creature scooped up the sleeping bag, with the man in it, and slung it over his shoulder. For the next week, the prospector was held captive by a Bigfoot family. In addition to the one that captured him, he said, there were two other Bigfoot creatures. The three behaved as father, mother and child.

During that week, the Bigfoot creatures seemed to be observing the man. He studied them, too. He concluded that they were not apes, but primitive human beings. They even talked to each other in a simple language.

The prospector finally managed to escape and find his way back to civilization. He didn't tell anyone about his experience. When asked why, he claimed that he was afraid people would laugh at him. Supposedly, the man kept his secret for thirty-three years. As more and more Bigfoot sightings were reported, he decided to come forward with his story.

New Bigfoot sightings are still reported from time to time. No one knows exactly what a Bigfoot is or where it comes from. But several theories have been proposed. The most popular one is that Bigfoot is a primitive creature, half human and half ape. People who embrace this theory think that millions of years ago there were many such creatures. They believe that a few of their descendants are still around. At first it may seem that such creatures could not possibly have stayed so well hidden in today's crowded world. But there are still some great, dense forests in North America.

Another explanation is offered for Bigfoot's ability to avoid people. Some folks think that Bigfoot is a visitor from outer space. In this age of space adventure movies, it is not hard to imagine Bigfoot coming to earth from another planet. In fact, whenever there is a Bigfoot sighting, there also seems to be an increase in the number of UFO sightings in the area.

Despite the many theories (some pretty farfetched), stories, and sightings of Bigfoot, we still have no proof that any such creature exists. Nobody has ever captured one. No Bigfoot bodies have ever been found. What we do have are many photographs of a beast that fits the descriptions, and many plaster casts of huge footprints. We also have a few feet of movie film showing a large hairy creature walking through the woods. The film was made by two men in a forest in northern California in 1967. One of the men had been a Bigfoot fan for years. He wanted to capture the creature on film. The men claim that they did find a Bigfoot. (At least they have some film of a hairy, upright creature.) In the film, the Bigfoot looks very much like a man walking around in a monster suit. Film experts and scientists who saw the movie couldn't tell whether this Bigfoot was real or a fake.

Is there a Bigfoot or isn't there? No one is sure. The photographs and plaster casts could be fakes. Or maybe they're real? Well, certainly the people in Skamamia, Washington, seem convinced. There have been so many Bigfoot sightings around Skamamia that the town has passed a Bigfoot law. In Skamamia, it is illegal to kill a Bigfoot. Punishment for the crime is a fine of $10,000 and five years in jail. As yet, no one has been caught breaking that law. ■

If you have been timed while reading this selection, enter your reading time below. Then turn to the Words per Minute table on page 154 and look up your reading speed (words per minute). Enter your reading speed on the graph on page 156.

READING TIME: Unit 4

_____ : _____
Minutes   *Seconds*

How well did you read?

- *Answer the four types of questions that follow. The directions for each type of question tell you how to mark your answers.*

- *When you have finished all four exercises, check your work by using the answer key on page 150. For each right answer, put a check mark (✓) on the line beside the box. For each wrong answer, write the correct answer on the line.*

- *For scoring each exercise, follow the directions below the questions.*

A FINDING THE MAIN IDEA

Look at the three statements below. One expresses the main idea of the story you just read. A good main idea statement answers two questions: it tells *who* or *what* is the subject of the story, and it answers the understood question *does what?* or *is what?* Another statement is *too broad*, it is vague and doesn't tell much about the topic of the story. The third statement is *too narrow*, it tells about only one part of the story.

Match the statements with the three answer choices below by writing the letter of each answer in the box in front of the statement it goes with.

M—Main Idea   **B—Too Broad**   **N—Too Narrow**

_____ ☐ 1. Legends of a creature called Bigfoot have been widespread in North America for a very long time.

_____ ☐ 2. Although many people have claimed to have seen a Bigfoot, no bodies have ever been found.

_____ ☐ 3. Though there have been hundreds of reports of sightings of a large, hairy creature known as Bigfoot, there is no proof of Bigfoot's existence.

_____ Score 15 points for a correct *M* answer

_____ Score 5 points for each correct *B* or *N* answer

_____ TOTAL SCORE: Finding the Main Idea

B RECALLING FACTS

How well do you remember the facts in the story you just read?
Put an x in the box in front of the correct answer to each of the
multiple-choice questions below.

1. The miners who reported an encounter with a Bigfoot
   in 1924 were in
   ___ ☐ a. California.
   ___ ☐ b. Washington State.
   ___ ☐ c. Skamamia.

2. The prospector captured by a Bigfoot
   ___ ☐ a. hid from the creature in his sleeping bag.
   ___ ☐ b. escaped by rolling up in a sleeping bag.
   ___ ☐ c. was asleep in his sleeping bag when captured.

3. The prospector claimed that he delayed reporting his
   experience because he
   ___ ☐ a. wanted to write a book about it.
   ___ ☐ b. thought nobody would believe it.
   ___ ☐ c. was afraid of the creatures.

4. No one has ever
   ___ ☐ a. taken a picture of a Bigfoot.
   ___ ☐ b. found a Bigfoot body.
   ___ ☐ c. found Bigfoot footprints.

5. Skamamia, Washington,
   ___ ☐ a. offers a reward of $10,000 for capturing a
   Bigfoot.
   ___ ☐ b. offers $10,000 for a Bigfoot, dead or alive.
   ___ ☐ c. has made it illegal to kill a Bigfoot.

Score 5 points for each correct answer

___ TOTAL SCORE: Recalling Facts

C MAKING INFERENCES

An inference is a judgment that is made or an idea that is
arrived at based on facts or on information that is given. You
make an inference when you understand something that is *not*
stated directly, but that is *implied,* or suggested by the facts that
are given.

Below are five statements that are judgments or ideas that
have been arrived at from the facts of the story. Write the letter
C in the box in front of each statement that is a correct inference. Write the letter *F* in front of each faulty inference.

C—Correct Inference   **F—Faulty Inference**

___ ☐ 1. The Mount St. Helens miners were cautious men.

___ ☐ 2. If there is such a creature as Bigfoot, it usually
   doesn't want anything to do with people.

___ ☐ 3. The people of Skamamia, Washington, like the
   idea that Bigfoot may live near them.

___ ☐ 4. Film experts concluded that the 1967 movie of
   Bigfoot was really a man in an ape suit.

___ ☐ 5. The prospector was probably telling the truth
   about being held captive by a Bigfoot family,
   because he had no reason to make up such a
   story.

Score 5 points for each correct answer

___ TOTAL SCORE: Making Inferences

D USING WORDS PRECISELY

Each of the numbered sentences below contains an underlined word or phrase from the story you have just read. Under the sentence are three definitions. One has the *same* meaning as the underlined word or phrase, one has *almost the same* meaning, and one has the *opposite* meaning. Match the definitions with the three answer choices by writing the letter that stands for each answer in the box in front of the definition it goes with.

S—Same   A—Almost the Same   O—Opposite

1. A sickening odor <u>emanates from</u> his hairy body.

   ____ ☐ a. grows from

   ____ ☐ b. goes into

   ____ ☐ c. comes from

2. All four men saw it plunge over the <u>precipice</u>.

   ____ ☐ a. cliff

   ____ ☐ b. plain

   ____ ☐ c. mountains

3. People who <u>embrace</u> this theory think that millions of years ago there were many such creatures, and that a few of their descendants are still around.

   ____ ☐ a. select

   ____ ☐ b. accept

   ____ ☐ c. reject

4. But there are still some great, <u>dense</u> forests in North America.

   ____ ☐ a. full

   ____ ☐ b. thick

   ____ ☐ c. open

5. Although no one knows exactly what a Bigfoot is or where it comes from, several theories have been <u>proposed</u>.

   ____ ☐ a. put forward

   ____ ☐ b. advised

   ____ ☐ c. held back

____ Score 3 points for each correct S answer

____ Score 1 point for each correct A or O answer

____ TOTAL SCORE: Using Words Precisely

● *Enter the four total scores in the spaces below, and add them together to find your Critical Reading Score. Then record your Critical Reading Score on the graph on page 157.*

_____ Finding the Main Idea
_____ Recalling Facts
_____ Making Inferences
_____ Using Words Precisely
_____ CRITICAL READING SCORE: Unit 4

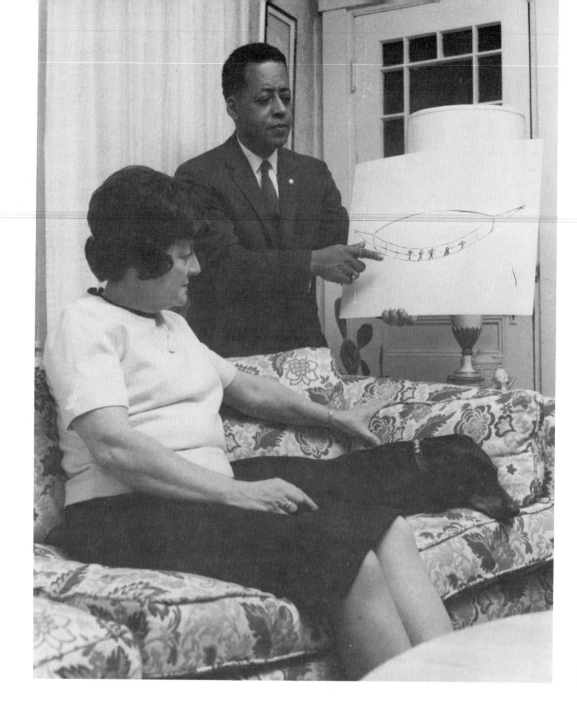

Betty and Barney Hill look like average people, but they claim to have had an experience that was far from average. They say that on the night of September 19, 1961, they were taken aboard a flying saucer. At left, Barney is showing a drawing of the saucer. The Hills say that the aliens followed and then abducted them on a dark stretch of road in the White Mountains of New Hampshire. Below is an artist's interpretation of one of the creatures, as Betty and Barney described them.

Has Earth Been Visited by Creatures from UFOs?

It was a lovely autumn evening in 1961. Betty and Barney Hill were driving down through New Hampshire on their way home from vacation. At about ten o'clock, they reached a particularly lonely section of highway. Suddenly the couple noticed a bright object in the sky. It appeared to be moving along behind their car. It was not getting any closer, but neither did it show any signs of fading away. Delsey, the Hills' dog, was also in the car. The bright object seemed to make Delsey nervous. The couple decided to stop the car so they could walk the dog.

Barney got out of the car and looked up at the sky through a pair of binoculars. The bright object was still there, hovering overhead. But Barney couldn't figure out what it was. After staring at it for a moment, he put away his binoculars and took Delsey for a short walk. As he strolled down the deserted road, he tried not to think about the strange object in the sky. But when he and Betty put the dog back in the car and began driving again, the bright object resumed following them.

At midnight the object was still trailing along behind their car. Once again Barney stopped the car to take a look. That time he could discern its shape. It looked like a plane of some sort, but it didn't have any wings. Barney saw colored lights flashing on and off. Then all at once a wave of panic flooded over him. He had the sudden impression that even as he stood watching the object, it was watching him. Frightened, Barney jumped back into his car and drove away.

The next thing Barney knew, he was sitting behind the wheel of his car, parked on a completely different stretch of road. According to a road sign, he and Betty were about thirty-five miles from their last stop. Barney had no memory of driving to that spot. He had no idea how they had gotten there and neither had Betty. According to Betty's watch, two hours had passed since they had stopped to look at the mysterious light. It didn't make sense. Had they driven for those two hours? If so, why had they only gone thirty-five miles? And why couldn't they remember doing it? Shaken, Barney and Betty did not talk much on the rest of their trip home.

With their vacation over, the Hills' lives went back to normal. Soon, however, Betty began to have terrible nightmares. She dreamed that she and Barney were kidnapped by creatures from another planet. Barney, too, began to have problems. He had trouble falling asleep. He also began to feel tired and to suffer from headaches. When his doctor couldn't figure out what was wrong, he referred Barney to a psychiatrist. The psychiatrist, Dr. Benjamin Simon, thought that perhaps Barney's problems were caused by a past event that was troubling him. Neither Barney nor Betty could remember any such event. But Dr. Simon claimed that memories of unpleasant events sometimes become deeply buried in people's minds. He also believed that hypnosis might be able to uncover such events. He decided to hypnotize Barney and Betty, one at a time.

Under hypnosis, each related the same story. They talked of that night in New Hampshire when they had seen a strange object in the sky. They told Dr. Simon about Barney's sudden panic as he stared up at the sky. They explained that they had tried to drive away but had gotten lost and ended up driving down a side road. Ahead on the road, they saw flashing lights. People were standing in the road, signaling to them.

Under hypnosis, the Hills remembered thinking that there had been some sort of accident. They thought that the people were police officers signaling them to stop. Only after they stopped did they see that the figures were not police at all. In fact, they were not even human. They were strange, alien creatures who stood next to a spaceship. As the Hills looked at the spaceship, they realized that it was the object they had been seeing in the sky. They recognized the bright lights.

Still in a hypnotic trance, Barney told how he had been dragged into the spaceship. Betty recalled that she had simply walked in. Inside, the Hills were told that they wouldn't be hurt. The aliens undressed them and examined them with various instruments. After an hour or so aboard the spacecraft, Barney and Betty were returned to their car. There they found Delsey, their dog, sleeping.

When Dr. Simon asked the Hills to describe the aliens, they both gave the same description. The creatures wore black jackets. Their bodies looked human, but their faces were more like those of insects. Betty said that they had mouths with no lips, and large, slanting eyes. Barney, too, remembered those eyes. Even now, months later, he was terrified of them. He pleaded with Dr. Simon, "Those eyes. They're in my brain. Please! Can't I wake up?"

Before Dr. Simon ended Betty's hypnotic trance, she remembered one other thing. She recalled seeing a star map on a wall in the spacecraft. After the doctor woke her, she drew a picture of the map. It contained twenty-six stars, each with planets orbiting them.

Betty knew nothing at all about astronomy, so Dr. Simon was surprised to learn that all twenty-six of those stars did exist. Furthermore, she had drawn the stars in the right size and position in relation to one another. Although scientists have not yet discovered planets around those stars, some believe that they may well exist. The stars on Betty's map are the kind that often do have planets.

The Hills had been ordinary people, but their tale of space adventure made them famous. A writer named John Fuller, who was an expert on UFOs, wrote a book about them. Dr. Simon had recorded the story Barney had told while under hypnosis. John Fuller quoted from those tapes. The result was a dramatic book. The Hills became popular speakers, telling their story on radio and television.

The story is certainly an exciting one. The question is, did it really happen? There is no doubt that the Hills are honest people. Under hypnosis they were clearly telling what they believed was the truth. But nobody else saw the spaceship or the aliens. Nearby radar tracking stations did not pick up any strange aircraft the night of the Hills' adventure.

Dr. Simon doesn't believe that the Hills really went aboard a spaceship. His explanation is that the Hills did see a bright object in the sky. They became frightened and convinced themselves that they'd seen a spaceship. Some time later, Betty Hill began having nightmares. In her dreams she was taken aboard a spaceship. Again and again Betty told her dreams to Barney. After a while he began to believe in them. When Dr. Simon placed the Hills under hypnosis, they both told the story of Betty's nightmares.

We will probably never be sure what really happened. Every explanation leaves some questions unanswered. Perhaps the space people were products of Betty Hill's imagination. But could it also be that on that dark night in 1961 Betty and Barney Hill became the first humans ever to board an alien spaceship? ■

If you have been timed while reading this selection, enter your reading time below. Then turn to the Words per Minute table on page 154 and look up your reading speed (words per minute). Enter your reading speed on the graph on page 156.

READING TIME: Unit 5

——————— : ———————
Minutes   *Seconds*

How well did you read?

- *Answer the four types of questions that follow. The directions for each type of question tell you how to mark your answers.*

- *When you have finished all four exercises, check your work by using the answer key on page 150. For each right answer, put a check mark (✓) on the line beside the box. For each wrong answer, write the correct answer on the line.*

- *For scoring each exercise, follow the directions below the questions.*

A FINDING THE MAIN IDEA

Look at the three statements below. One expresses the main idea of the story you just read. A good main idea statement answers two questions: it tells *who* or *what* is the subject of the story, and it answers the understood question *does what?* or *is what?* Another statement is *too broad*, it is vague and doesn't tell much about the topic of the story. The third statement is *too narrow*, it tells about only one part of the story.

Match the statements with the three answer choices below by writing the letter of each answer in the box in front of the statement it goes with.

M—Main Idea   B—Too Broad   N—Too Narrow

_____ ☐ 1. Barney and Betty Hill claimed that they had seen beings from outer space.

_____ ☐ 2. Betty and Barney Hill claimed that in the fall of 1961 they were taken aboard an alien spaceship.

_____ ☐ 3. The psychiatrist who hypnotized Betty and Barney thought that the experience they described took place only in Betty's dreams.

_____ Score 15 points for a correct *M* answer

_____ Score 5 points for each correct *B* or *N* answer

_____ TOTAL SCORE: Finding the Main Idea

B RECALLING FACTS

How well do you remember the facts in the story you just read? Put an *x* in the box in front of the correct answer to each of the multiple-choice questions below.

1. The Hills first noticed the spaceship
   - ☐ a. when they stopped to walk their dog.
   - ☐ b. when they viewed the sky through binoculars.
   - ☐ c. while they were driving.

2. After their adventure, Barney
   - ☐ a. began to have nightmares.
   - ☐ b. had trouble staying awake.
   - ☐ c. had trouble falling asleep.

3. Dr. Benjamin Simon hypnotized the Hills so that
   - ☐ a. they'd be able to recall things they couldn't remember otherwise.
   - ☐ b. he could communicate with the aliens through Barney.
   - ☐ c. he could find out why Betty had nightmares.

4. When the Hills first saw the creatures from the strange craft, they thought they were
   - ☐ a. insects with strange eyes.
   - ☐ b. police officers.
   - ☐ c. people who had been in an accident.

5. Dr. Simon believed that the Hills
   - ☐ a. went aboard a spaceship.
   - ☐ b. convinced themselves that they had gone aboard a spaceship.
   - ☐ c. saw a spaceship but never went aboard it.

Score 5 points for each correct answer

_____ TOTAL SCORE: Recalling Facts

C MAKING INFERENCES

An inference is a judgment that is made or an idea that is arrived at based on facts or on information that is given. You make an inference when you understand something that is *not* stated directly, but that is *implied,* or suggested by the facts that are given.

Below are five statements that are judgments or ideas that have been arrived at from the facts of the story. Write the letter *C* in the box in front of each statement that is a correct inference. Write the letter *F* in front of each faulty inference.

C—Correct Inference   F—Faulty Inference

1. Betty lied about not knowing anything about astronomy.

2. The Hills believed that they had really gone into a spaceship.

3. The Hills enjoyed the fame their story brought them.

4. Dr. Simon himself convinced the Hills, under hypnosis, that they had been in a spaceship.

5. The Hills only imagined they saw a bright object in the sky.

Score 5 points for each correct answer

_____ TOTAL SCORE: Making Inferences

D USING WORDS PRECISELY

Each of the numbered sentences below contains an underlined word or phrase from the story you have just read. Under the sentence are three definitions. One has the *same* meaning as the underlined word or phrase, one has *almost the same* meaning, and one has the *opposite* meaning. Match the definitions with the three answer choices by writing the letter that stands for each answer in the box in front of the definition it goes with.

S—Same   A—Almost the Same   O—Opposite

1. That time he could <u>discern</u> its shape.

   ____ ☐ a. guess at

   ____ ☐ b. not tell

   ____ ☐ c. make out

2. But when he and Betty put the dog back in the car and began driving again, the bright object <u>resumed</u> following them.

   ____ ☐ a. left off

   ____ ☐ b. continued

   ____ ☐ c. started up again

3. <u>Shaken</u>, Barney and Betty did not talk much on the rest of their trip home.

   ____ ☐ a. disturbed

   ____ ☐ b. unconcerned

   ____ ☐ c. distressed

4. When his doctor couldn't figure out what was wrong, he <u>referred</u> Barney to a psychiatrist.

   ____ ☐ a. sent

   ____ ☐ b. advised against going

   ____ ☐ c. recommended

5. Under hypnosis, each <u>related</u> the same story.

   ____ ☐ a. described

   ____ ☐ b. told

   ____ ☐ c. kept quiet about

____ Score 3 points for each correct *S* answer

____ Score 1 point for each correct *A* or *O* answer

____ TOTAL SCORE: Using Words Precisely

● *Enter the four total scores in the spaces below, and add them together to find your Critical Reading Score. Then record your Critical Reading Score on the graph on page 157.*

_____ Finding the Main Idea

_____ Recalling Facts

_____ Making Inferences

_____ Using Words Precisely

_____ CRITICAL READING SCORE: Unit 5

Hercules, half mortal and half god, was the strongest man in the world. But even he feared that the tasks set before him were impossible. How would he kill the Nemean lion, which could not be harmed by any weapon? Still worse, how would he get into the underworld and capture the terrible three-headed hound of hell? With no plan to guide him, but determined to accomplish the deeds, Hercules set out. There was no other way to make up for the horrible thing he had done.

The Nemean Lion and the Hound of Hell

It was late at night in the town of Thebes in ancient Greece. A young woman named Alcena had just put her baby son, Hercules, to bed. Suddenly she heard a strange noise coming from the baby's room. She rushed in to a shocking sight. Her infant son was sitting up in his crib, grasping a dead snake in each hand. Poison still dripped from the fangs of the serpents. The snakes were large and strong, but little Hercules had managed to strangle them with his bare hands. As his mother stared in amazement, he gleefully held up the dead snakes for her to see. From that moment on, it was clear that Hercules was no ordinary child.

Hercules got his extraordinary powers from his father. His mother was mortal, but his father was Zeus, king of the gods. Zeus was married to a goddess named Hera, who was terribly jealous of her husband's half-mortal child. It was Hera who sent the snakes to the nursery to kill Hercules. But even at such a tender age, Hercules was strong enough to protect himself.

Hercules was given a superior education. Because he was the son of Zeus, he was taught by the greatest men of his time. Even the gods themselves aided in his instruction. He was taught to use weapons, to wrestle, and to shoot with a bow and arrow. He was also exposed to literature and music.

By the time Hercules had grown to manhood, he was the strongest person on earth. He married a beautiful woman and soon was the father of three sons. Meanwhile, Hera had not forgotten him. Throughout the years, her hatred for him had grown. Finally, when Hercules' sons were still small, Hera decided on a plan. She sent to Hercules a sickness that caused him to go mad. In his madness, he imagined that his wife and children were his enemies, and he killed them.

When the madness passed, Hercules realized what he had done. Stricken with grief, he went to a priestess and asked her advice. The priestess told Hercules that his soul would once again be at peace only if he performed some great deeds to atone for the wrong he had done. She told him to go to the king of a distant city. The king would assign him certain tasks. After completing those tasks, he would be freed from guilt.

Hercules hurried to the king's palace. When he got there, the king described twelve tasks that he would have to accomplish. They all seemed impossible. Hercules was anxious to find peace, however, so he agreed to attempt them.

His first task was to kill and skin the Nemean lion. This was no ordinary lion, but a beast of tremendous size with a coat that could not be pierced by any weapon. Neither iron nor bronze nor stone had any effect on the beast's hide. How then to kill it?

Hercules entered the lair of the Nemean lion, but found it empty. He sat down to wait, and soon he saw the enormous creature approaching, its body spattered with the blood of its recent victims. Hercules steadied his bow and shot a flight of arrows at the lion. But the arrows did no good; they simply rebounded off the beast's thick hide. As the lion drew closer, it licked the blood from its mouth and yawned in Hercules' face. Hercules then drew his sword and thrust it at the lion, but that weapon, too, proved useless. When the sword met the lion's hide, the blade bent as if made of tin. With panic rising in his chest, Hercules grabbed his club and began to beat the lion over the head. Although that annoyed the lion and made its ears ring, the club did not really injure the animal. When Hercules tried to strike the lion with more force, the club shattered.

Hercules could think of only one other thing to do. He lunged toward the lion and grabbed it around the throat with his bare hands. The lion fought back with all its energy. With its teeth, it ripped off one of Hercules' fingers. Still Hercules held on, managing finally to strangle the beast to death.

Next Hercules had to find a way to remove the hide from the dead lion. Even in death, the hide of the Nemean lion was invulnerable to knives. As Hercules looked at the body, he had an idea. Using one of the lion's own razor-sharp claws, he was able to pierce the hide and skin the body.

Hercules carried the lion's carcass back to the king. Then he set out to perform the remaining tasks. Although all called for great strength and cunning, Hercules managed to complete them one by one. Soon he was left with only one task. It was by far the most dangerous of all. He was obliged to descend into Hades to capture Cerberus (SER-buh-rus), the Hound of Hell.

Cerberus was a three-headed dog that stood guard at the gates of Hell. Each of the three heads was surrounded by a mane of hissing serpents. The serpents were constantly coiling and uncoiling, thrusting out in all directions. The hound's tail was as dangerous as its heads, for it ended in a sharp blade topped with a deadly barb. When attacked, Cerberus would whip its tail around to ward off its enemy.

Before Hercules could consider how best to confront the Hound of Hell, he had to get into the underworld. No living mortal had ever gone there before. In preparation for his journey, Hercules underwent a ritual cleansing. He also prayed and made sacrifices to the gods. Then he set out for Hades.

After traveling a long way, Hercules finally reached the River Styx. The river separates the land of the living from the land of the dead. He persuaded a ghostly boatman to ferry him across. On the shore of Hades, he was met by many ghosts. At first Hercules was frightened, but he soon realized that the dead could not harm him.

To calm the ghosts, Hercules, according to custom, decided to make an animal sacrifice to them. Because he needed animal blood for the sacrifice, he slaughtered one of the underworld cattle. On seeing that, the herdsman of Hell, who looked after the cattle, challenged Hercules to a wrestling match. Hercules grabbed the herdsman tightly around the chest and squeezed so hard that he broke the herdsman's ribs. He would have squeezed the man to death, but the queen of the underworld stepped in. She told Hercules that in return for sparing her herdsman, he could have the Hound of Hell. "Cerberus is yours," she said, "but only if you can master him without using your club or your arrows."

Hercules found Cerberus chained to the gates of one of the rivers of Hell. When the dog saw Hercules approach, the snakes on its heads began spitting poison. Ignoring the snakes, Hercules gripped the dog by the throat from which all three heads rose. Cerberus whipped its barbed tail at Hercules, but still Hercules did not let go. He swept off an animal skin that covered his shoulders and threw it over the dog's three heads. The beast became so entangled in the lion skin that it was soon lying helpless at Hercules' feet.

Hercules bound the dog in chains and began dragging it up from Hell. As they traveled, Cerberus resisted the bright light of earth. All three of its heads started barking and snarling. But Hercules just gathered the dog up in his arms and kept on. As he retraced his steps to the land of the living, his heart was light. His guilt over murdering his family was erased at last. ■

If you have been timed while reading this selection, enter your reading time below. Then turn to the Words per Minute table on page 154 and look up your reading speed (words per minute). Enter your reading speed on the graph on page 156.

READING TIME: Unit 6

_____ : _____
Minutes   *Seconds*

How well did you read?

- *Answer the four types of questions that follow. The directions for each type of question tell you how to mark your answers.*

- *When you have finished all four exercises, check your work by using the answer key on page 150. For each right answer, put a check mark (✔) on the line beside the box. For each wrong answer, write the correct answer on the line.*

- *For scoring each exercise, follow the directions below the questions.*

A FINDING THE MAIN IDEA

Look at the three statements below. One expresses the main idea of the story you just read. A good main idea statement answers two questions: it tells *who* or *what* is the subject of the story, and it answers the understood question *does what?* or *is what?* Another statement is *too broad*, it is vague and doesn't tell much about the topic of the story. The third statement is *too narrow*, it tells about only one part of the story.

Match the statements with the three answer choices below by writing the letter of each answer in the box in front of the statement it goes with.

M—Main Idea   **B—Too Broad**   **N—Too Narrow**

____ ☐ 1. Hercules had to perform twelve terrible tasks, and the most difficult of them were the slaying of the Nemean lion and the capturing of the Hound of Hell.

____ ☐ 2. While in a state of madness brought on by the jealous goddess Hera, Hercules murdered his wife and children.

____ ☐ 3. Hercules performed many incredibly difficult deeds that a mere mortal would never have been able to do.

____ Score 15 points for a correct *M* answer
____ Score 5 points for each correct *B* or *N* answer
____ TOTAL SCORE: Finding the Main Idea

B RECALLING FACTS

How well do you remember the facts in the story you just read? Put an *x* in the box in front of the correct answer to each of the multiple-choice questions below.

1. Hercules killed his wife and children because
   - ____ ☐ a. Zeus told him to.
   - ____ ☐ b. Hera made him go temporarily mad.
   - ____ ☐ c. the king ordered him to.

2. Hercules was
   - ____ ☐ a. half mortal and half god.
   - ____ ☐ b. the son of Zeus and Hera.
   - ____ ☐ c. the king of the gods.

3. Hercules was finally able to skin the Nemean lion using
   - ____ ☐ a. a bronze knife.
   - ____ ☐ b. one of the lion's claws.
   - ____ ☐ c. a silver dagger.

4. The Hound of Hell had
   - ____ ☐ a. five heads.
   - ____ ☐ b. nine heads.
   - ____ ☐ c. three heads.

5. Hercules got into a wrestling match in Hades because he
   - ____ ☐ a. killed some cattle.
   - ____ ☐ b. attacked the herdsman of Hell.
   - ____ ☐ c. insulted some ghosts.

Score 5 points for each correct answer

____ TOTAL SCORE: Recalling Facts

C MAKING INFERENCES

An inference is a judgment that is made or an idea that is arrived at based on facts or on information that is given. You make an inference when you understand something that is *not* stated directly, but that is *implied*, or suggested by the facts that are given.

Below are five statements that are judgments or ideas that have been arrived at from the facts of the story. Write the letter *C* in the box in front of each statement that is a correct inference. Write the letter *F* in front of each faulty inference.

C—Correct Inference   F—Faulty Inference

- ____ ☐ 1. Hercules knew his father was Zeus.

- ____ ☐ 2. The king was certain that Hercules could accomplish the twelve tasks he assigned him.

- ____ ☐ 3. When Hercules went to the den of the Nemean lion, he had a plan for killing it.

- ____ ☐ 4. The herdsman of Hell and his cattle were important to the queen of Hades.

- ____ ☐ 5. Once he was released from Hades, Cerberus was glad to be in the land of the living.

Score 5 points for each correct answer

____ TOTAL SCORE: Making Inferences

D USING WORDS PRECISELY

Each of the numbered sentences below contains an underlined word or phrase from the story you have just read. Under the sentence are three definitions. One has the *same* meaning as the underlined word or phrase, one has *almost the same* meaning, and one has the *opposite* meaning. Match the definitions with the three answer choices by writing the letter that stands for each answer in the box in front of the definition it goes with.

S—Same   A—Almost the Same   O—Opposite

1. The priestess told Hercules that his soul would once again be at peace only if he performed some great deeds to atone for the wrong he had done.

____ ☐ a. prove that he had good reason

____ ☐ b. make up for

____ ☐ c. apologize for

2. Hercules then drew his sword and thrust it at the lion, but that weapon, too, proved useless.

____ ☐ a. jabbed

____ ☐ b. pushed with force

____ ☐ c. pulled it back from

3. Even in death, the hide of the Nemean lion was invulnerable to knives.

____ ☐ a. incapable of being injured by

____ ☐ b. open to danger by

____ ☐ c. difficult to penetrate

4. He was obliged to descend into Hades to capture Cerberus, the Hound of Hell.

____ ☐ a. was forced to

____ ☐ b. did not have to

____ ☐ c. had to

5. When attacked, Cerberus would whip its tail around to ward off its enemy.

____ ☐ a. drive back

____ ☐ b. push away

____ ☐ c. attract

____ Score 3 points for each correct *S* answer

____ Score 1 point for each correct *A* or *O* answer

____ TOTAL SCORE: Using Words Precisely

● *Enter the four total scores in the spaces below, and add them together to find your Critical Reading Score. Then record your Critical Reading Score on the graph on page 157.*

_____ Finding the Main Idea

_____ Recalling Facts

_____ Making Inferences

_____ Using Words Precisely

_____ CRITICAL READING SCORE: Unit 6

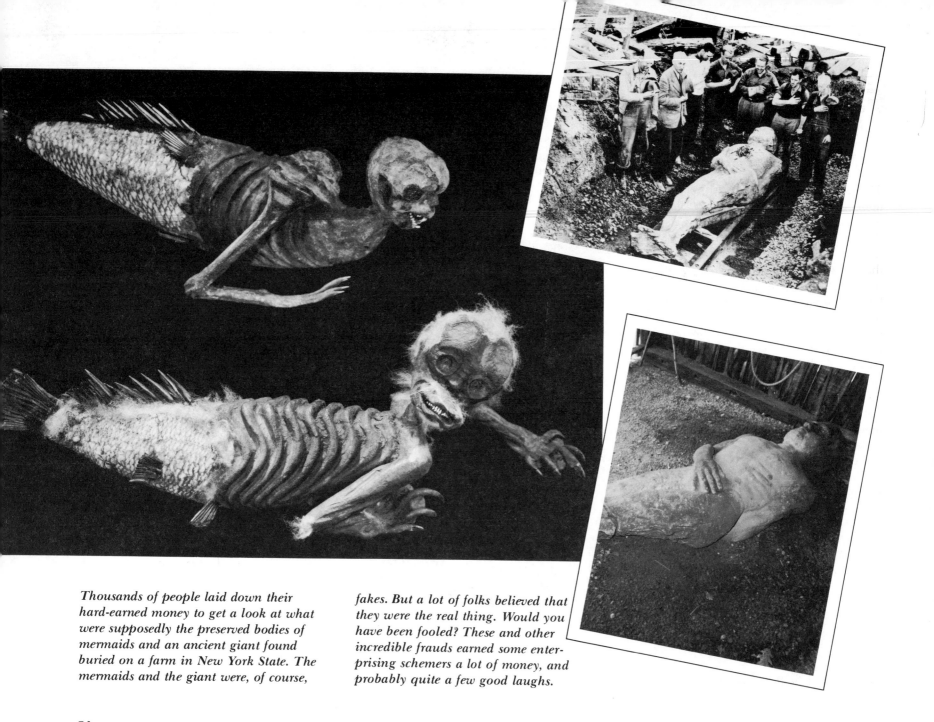

Thousands of people laid down their hard-earned money to get a look at what were supposedly the preserved bodies of mermaids and an ancient giant found buried on a farm in New York State. The mermaids and the giant were, of course, fakes. But a lot of folks believed that they were the real thing. Would you have been fooled? These and other incredible frauds earned some enterprising schemers a lot of money, and probably quite a few good laughs.

Fabulous Fakes

The two workmen had been digging for hours under the hot autumn sun. Although digging a well was hard work, the job had been going smoothly. The workers were pleased with the progress they were making. Suddenly, though, they heard a sharp "Clang!" One of the shovels had struck something. At first the men thought they had hit a rock. As they started to dig around the object, however, they found that it had a strange shape. Growing anxious about what they would find, they began to dig frantically. Soon they unearthed a foot, then a leg, then the rest of a body. It was a man. But what a man! He was ten feet, four and a half inches tall, and he was made entirely of stone!

The well diggers were astonished. They knew that according to the Bible there had once been giants on the earth. So they thought it was logical that the remains of those giants should lie somewhere in the earth. But they were amazed to think that they had found the first body there on a New York farm in the mid 1800s.

As they stared at the stone man, the workmen grew more and more excited. They were sure that they would become famous. After all, they had just made one of the greatest scientific discoveries of the nineteenth century. Surely this giant fossil was the most important find in the history of paleontology!

There was only one thing wrong with the workmen's discovery: the stone giant was one of the biggest frauds of all time.

The stone giant was actually the creation of a man named George Hull. Hull, who made cigars from the tobacco he grew on his farm, lived in Binghamton, New York. He had dreamed up the idea of a stone giant while visiting his sister. During the visit, he had gone to church. The preacher spoke about the giants mentioned in the Bible. From the sermon, Hull got the notion of burying a stone man and then promoting it as a petrified Biblical giant.

Hull convinced his business partner, H. B. Martin, to help him with the hoax. First the two men obtained a five-ton block of gypsum. Then they hired two sculptors to carve the statue. Hull was the model for the figure. It took the sculptors three months of hard work to finish the job. When they were through, Hull began his own work on the statue. Using a darning needle, he pounded thousands of tiny holes into the soft stone. This made the giant's skin look like it had pores. Then Hull "aged" the giant figure by pouring sulfuric acid all over it.

The completed giant was crated and shipped by rail to a train station near a farm in Cardiff, New York. When it arrived there, Hull had the crate placed in a wagon. It took four horses to pull the heavy load to the farm in Cardiff. Once Hull had the stone man on the farm, he buried it. He let a year pass. Then hired the unsuspecting workmen to dig a well in the spot where the giant was buried.

Newspapers hailed the giant as the Eighth Wonder of the World. They called it the "American Goliath." Hull placed the giant on display in a tent and charged fifty cents admission to view it. In those days, fifty cents was a full day's pay for the average worker. Despite the high price, as many as five hundred people paid to see the giant every weekday. One Sunday, more than two thousand people paid it a visit.

Hull was anxious to sell the statue before it was revealed as a fake. He soon sold three-quarters of his rights to some businessmen. They moved the figure to nearby Syracuse. The new partners thought that the giant would draw an even bigger crowd in that large city, and they were right. Thousands viewed the figure and went away marveling over it. But O. C. Marsh, a young paleontologist from Yale University, took one look at the giant and declared it a "decided humbug."

At that point, George Hull confessed to the entire hoax. But even though the whole world then knew it to be a fake, people kept going to see the giant. The great showman P. T. Barnum had a copy of the statue made, and he put it on exhibit in his museum. People even flocked there to see what they knew to be a fake of a fake. Today, George Hull's giant still draws crowds. The Cardiff Giant, as it came to be called, is one of the exhibits at the museum of the New York State Historical Association in Cooperstown.

Are you amazed that people could be tricked into believing that Hull's stone statue was really the body of a giant? Then you will be truly astonished at the fakes known as "fur-bearing trout." Mounted specimens are sometimes exhibited at fairs. They can also be found in bars in Canada and across the northern United States. The people who display them explain that the unusual fish live only in deep water that is very cold. The fish adapted to their icy environment by growing fur for warmth. The deeper the water in which the fish are caught, the tricksters will tell you, the thicker their fur.

The truth is that taxidermists attached the fur to the bodies of dead trout. And though the furry trout look realistic, it is surprising that people believe the far-fetched stories about them.

Another outlandish creature is the "jackalope." This animal looks like a rabbit with antlers. It is said to be a rare species that is in danger of dying out. Like the fur-bearing trout, however, the antlered rabbit is a fake. It is made by attaching the antlers of an antelope to the body of a jackrabbit. Hence its name.

One other creature that has been the object of many hoaxes is the mermaid. Over the course of many centuries, sailors reported seeing mermaids frolicking in the open seas. Many of those seagoing men truly believed that they had seen ocean creatures with the heads and torsos of women and the lower bodies of fish. Eventually, some crooked taxidermists who knew how gullible people could be decided to cash in on the legends. They made up their own mermaid specimens and exhibited them for a fee. Historically, mermaids have been reported to be beautiful creatures about the size of women. The fake mermaids, however, were small and grotesque. That was because most of them were made up of the head, shoulders and chest of a shaved monkey joined to the body and tail of a fish. Other mermaid fakes were made by stitching the head and shoulders of an ape to the tail of a porpoise. Those "mermaids" were larger, but no less ugly.

It is almost unbelievable that people would fall for such outrageous fakes as the monkey mermaids, stone giant, fur-bearing trout and jackalope. But our imaginations can reach far beyond the world we live in. What we can imagine is often more exciting and interesting than the routine of our daily lives. The fakes provided food for people's imaginations. ∎

If you have been timed while reading this selection, enter your reading time below. Then turn to the Words per Minute table on page 154 and look up your reading speed (words per minute). Enter your reading speed on the graph on page 156.

READING TIME: Unit 7

_____ : _____
Minutes   Seconds

How well did you read?

- *Answer the four types of questions that follow. The directions for each type of question tell you how to mark your answers.*

- *When you have finished all four exercises, check your work by using the answer key on page 150. For each right answer, put a check mark (✔) on the line beside the box. For each wrong answer, write the correct answer on the line.*

- *For scoring each exercise, follow the directions below the questions.*

A FINDING THE MAIN IDEA

Look at the three statements below. One expresses the main idea of the story you just read. A good main idea statement answers two questions: it tells *who* or *what* is the subject of the story, and it answers the understood question *does what?* or *is what?* Another statement is *too broad,* it is vague and doesn't tell much about the topic of the story. The third statement is *too narrow,* it tells about only one part of the story.

Match the statements with the three answer choices below by writing the letter of each answer in the box in front of the statement it goes with.

M—Main Idea   B—Too Broad   N—Too Narrow

____ ☐ 1. The Cardiff Giant was a successful hoax that continues to attract interest.

____ ☐ 2. Over the years, many people have been fooled into believing that various fake creatures were real.

____ ☐ 3. There have always been a great number of people gullible enough to be fooled into believing outlandish things.

____ Score 15 points for a correct *M* answer

____ Score 5 points for each correct *B* or *N* answer

____ TOTAL SCORE: Finding the Main Idea

B RECALLING FACTS

How well do you remember the facts in the story you just read?
Put an x in the box in front of the correct answer to each of the
multiple-choice questions below.

1. Hull got the idea for making a stone giant from
   ____ ☐ a. reading his Bible.
   ____ ☐ b. listening to a preacher.
   ____ ☐ c. his business partner.

2. The model for the Cardiff Giant was
   ____ ☐ a. Hull.
   ____ ☐ b. Hull's sister.
   ____ ☐ c. Hull's partner.

3. The Cardiff Giant was carved by
   ____ ☐ a. Hull.
   ____ ☐ b. two well diggers.
   ____ ☐ c. two sculptors.

4. Fur-bearing trout are found
   ____ ☐ a. in both Binghamton and Syracuse, New York.
   ____ ☐ b. in the northern United States and Canada.
   ____ ☐ c. at a museum of the New York State Historical
                Association.

5. Jackalopes are made by combining
   ____ ☐ a. a jackrabbit and an antelope.
   ____ ☐ b. a monkey and a fish.
   ____ ☐ c. an ape and a porpoise.

Score 5 points for each correct answer

____ TOTAL SCORE: Recalling Facts

C MAKING INFERENCES

An inference is a judgment that is made or an idea that is
arrived at based on facts or on information that is given. You
make an inference when you understand something that is *not*
stated directly, but that is *implied*, or suggested by the facts that
are given.

Below are five statements that are judgments or ideas that
have been arrived at from the facts of the story. Write the letter
C in the box in front of each statement that is a correct inference. Write the letter *F* in front of each faulty inference.

C—Correct Inference   F—Faulty Inference

____ ☐ 1. If the people who found the Cardiff Giant had
            not known about and believed in the Biblical
            giants, they would not have believed that the
            statue was a giant.

____ ☐ 2. Fur-bearing trout really may exist in some
            unexplored areas of the ocean.

____ ☐ 3. Fur-bearing trout and jackalopes are made very
            skillfully.

____ ☐ 4. Though the Cardiff Giant was a fake, there once
            really were giants on the earth.

____ ☐ 5. People today could not be fooled by fake
            creatures.

Score 5 points for each correct answer

____ TOTAL SCORE: Making Inferences

D USING WORDS PRECISELY

Each of the numbered sentences below contains an underlined word or phrase from the story you have just read. Under the sentence are three definitions. One has the *same* meaning as the underlined word or phrase, one has *almost the same* meaning, and one has the *opposite* meaning. Match the definitions with the three answer choices by writing the letter that stands for each answer in the box in front of the definition it goes with.

S—Same   A—Almost the Same   O—Opposite

1. George Hull, who made cigars from the tobacco he grew on his farm in Binghamton, New York, had dreamed up the whole hoax.

____ ☐ a. an act intended to trick people

____ ☐ b. honest but incredible thing

____ ☐ c. joke

2. Newspapers hailed the giant as the Eighth Wonder of the World.

____ ☐ a. greeted

____ ☐ b. accepted

____ ☐ c. rejected

3. But O. C. Marsh took one look at the giant and declared it a "decided humbug."

____ ☐ a. joke

____ ☐ b. fraud

____ ☐ c. real thing

4. Many of those seagoing men truly believed that they had seen ocean creatures with the heads and torsos of women and the lower bodies of fish.

____ ☐ a. lower body

____ ☐ b. chest

____ ☐ c. upper body

5. Eventually, some crooked taxidermists who knew how gullible people could be, decided to cash in on the legends.

____ ☐ a. suspicious

____ ☐ b. easy to fool

____ ☐ c. silly

____ Score 3 points for each correct *S* answer
____ Score 1 point for each correct *A* or *O* answer

____ TOTAL SCORE: Using Words Precisely

● *Enter the four total scores in the spaces below, and add them together to find your Critical Reading Score. Then record your Critical Reading Score on the graph on page 157.*

_____ Finding the Main Idea
_____ Recalling Facts
_____ Making Inferences
_____ Using Words Precisely

_____ CRITICAL READING SCORE: Unit 7

Movie Monsters

Movies have been entertaining people since shortly before the turn of the century. Since one of the ways that people love to be entertained is by being scared to death, monster movies came into being when the industry was still quite young. Some of the most frightening monsters have been based on characters from fiction. Perhaps the most famous of these are Frankenstein's monster and Count Dracula. Other monsters, some of them famous and some doomed to obscurity because they were so ridiculous, were created especially for movies. They ranged from giant frogs and spiders to oozing blobs of slime. And let us not forget one of the most successful movie monsters of all time, the werewolf—a man who turns into a killer wolf when the moon is full.

The Hollywood relationship with the werewolf dates back to the late 1920s. At that time, artists in Germany were trying to express, in drama, music, painting and film, their inner feelings about life in a troubled world. Many of the movies that came out of the German art movement dealt with the notion of a "double." The idea was that everyone had a second, evil person deep within them. Using that theme, the Germans made scary films about people whose dark sides surfaced and made them perform awful deeds.

However, when the Nazis began to take power in the early 1930s, many of the German directors, cameramen and actors fled to the United States. There they went to work for the American movie companies. And they brought their techniques—stark black-and-white settings, shadows, mists and strange camera angles—to the making of horror films. Famous movies such as *Dracula, The Mummy,* and *Dr. Jekyll and Mr. Hyde* were made in 1931 and 1932 by Germans and Americans working together, all in the German style. *The Werewolf of London*, released in 1935, was perhaps the best werewolf movie to come out of that period.

In 1941, Lon Chaney, Jr., in *The Wolf Man* kicked off a second cycle of werewolf movies. *The Wolf Man* was a taxing movie for Chaney. Every morning before filming began, the renowned makeup artist Jack Pierce spent five hours applying the actor's chillingly convincing makeup. Sometimes the director wanted to show Chaney changing from human to wolf man. To accomplish that, little clumps of hair would be glued onto Chaney's face a few at a time. A few inches of film would be shot, then the camera would be stopped. More hair would be applied, and a few more pictures would be taken, and so on. By the end of the series

of pictures, Chaney had become the Wolf Man. The effect on screen was convincing—so convincing, in fact, that *The Wolf Man* is regarded by many as the best of the werewolf movies.

Unfortunately, the rest of the second cycle of horror movies lapsed into imitation, with titles such as *The Ghost of Frankenstein* and *The Mummy's Hand*. By 1957, the werewolf film had become even sillier, with Michael Landon (yes, *that* Michael Landon) starring in *I Was a Teenage Werewolf*. And in 1961 the song "New Ghoul in School" was the best thing about the otherwise forgettable *Werewolf in a Girl's Dormitory*.

Moviemakers had such great success with the traditional monsters that they decided to introduce some brand new monsters to the big screen. In 1958 came the first of three films based on a short story called *The Fly*. In that movie, a scientist develops a machine that can transport objects from place to place. After testing the machine, the scientist gets set to transport himself. Just as the transporter begins working, however, a fly happens to enter it. Before the scientist can stop the machine, he finds himself with the head of a fly. His own head is on the fly's body. At the movie's end, the scientist does away with himself by crushing the awful fly's head in a huge press. The fly with the human head meets an equally horrible end as a spider's dinner.

Two big developments in the monster movies of the 1950s were the introduction of monsters created by atomic explosions and of monsters from outer space. Just about a decade before, World War II had been ended with the first explosions of atomic bombs. Never before had human beings known such destructive force. People's fears about the terrible power that now existed began to be expressed in art, literature and films.

One of the first pictures based on the unknown dangers of the release of atomic energy was called *Them.* The villains of that movie are giant ants. They have grown to a size of fifteen feet as the result of an atomic explosion. Their winged queen has flown into a large city's system of unused water tunnels. There she has hatched her eggs and raised a whole nest of giant offspring.

The monstrous ants occasionally leave their nest to go out to forage. When they encounter people, the ants kill them with an injection of formic acid. The people in the city mount a campaign to destroy the giant insects. Scientists lead armies on a search for their nest. The search is unsuccessful. Finally, however, the movie's

The repulsive Jabba the Hutt, from **Return of the Jedi**, *is one of the most fantastic movie monsters ever created. As a character in a space fantasy, he is very much a monster of our times. The movie aliens of the fifties were of a much different sort, but they too reflected the era in which they were created. Movie monsters have a history that is as long as the history of movies themselves. And their development is tied, in many ways, to the history of science and technology, as well as to the changing focus of people's fears.*

heroes find and invade the ants' nest. They manage to rescue two children who have been trapped by the giant insects. Using flamethrowers, the heroes are also able to destroy the killer ants.

The Beast from 20,000 Fathoms is another movie that features atomic energy. The beast is awakened from its long sleep by an underwater nuclear explosion. This movie became the model for a series of films about monsters that resulted from atomic blasts. The enormous octopus in *It Came from Beneath* was created by an atomic explosion. So was the monstrous spider in *Tarantula*. The killer insect in *The Deadly Mantis* and the dinosaur of *The Giant Behemoth* were also products of atomic blasts.

By far the most famous of all atomic film monsters is Godzilla. *Godzilla, King of the Monsters,* was an enormous success for the Japanese monster movie industry. Godzilla is a sort of fat Tyrannosaurus with atomic breath. No weapon seems capable of preventing him from destroying Tokyo. Finally, a young Japanese scientist decides to sacrifice his own life to kill the beast. Flying a plane that carries a nuclear device, the scientist deliberately crashes into the monster.

The brave scientist seems to have died in vain, however. The moviemakers made too much money with Godzilla to let him die after just one film. They kept bringing him back in such movies as *Return of*

Godzilla, Godzilla Versus the Thing and *King Kong Versus Godzilla.*

The idea of space exploration had been touched on in the movies as early as 1902 in *A Trip to the Moon* by French film pioneer George Melies. And a few space movies were made in the twenties and thirties. But they were mostly space fantasies. One of the best, made in the 1930s, was *Buck Rogers in the Twenty-Fifth Century.*

In the 1950s, serious space exploration began. We still had no realistic idea, however, of what existed in the universe beyond our own planet. Were there strange creatures on other planets? Were they smarter than us? If they were, would they try to take over the Earth? All these ideas, and more, became the basis for science fiction space films. The movies reflected people's fears and imaginings about what might be out there. One of the best films of the sort was the 1956 movie *Invasion of the Body Snatchers*. It featured beings from another planet that took over the bodies of people living in a small U.S. town.

Space creatures are still with us, but they have largely gone back into the world of fantasy. The disgusting Jabba the Hutt, from *Return of the Jedi* is one of the most fantastic monsters ever made. His great, slobbering, shapeless form has no doubt won him a permanent place in the monster hall of fame.

Where will our monsters come from

in the future? No one knows for sure, of course. But it's likely that as both technology and space exploration advance, space-monster movies will advance, as well. It was advanced technology, in terms of new materials and special effects, that made Jabba the Hutt possible. He could not have been created twenty years ago.

As we move out into space more and more, exploring other worlds, our ideas of what space holds will surely change, as will our conception of our relationship to the rest of the universe. It's a safe bet that those changes in perception will be reflected in the monsters that are created for the movies. ■

If you have been timed while reading this selection, enter your reading time below. Then turn to the Words per Minute table on page 155 and look up your reading speed (words per minute). Enter your reading speed on the graph on page 156.

READING TIME: Unit 8

_____ : _____
Minutes   *Seconds*

How well did you read?

- *Answer the four types of questions that follow. The directions for each type of question tell you how to mark your answers.*

- *When you have finished all four exercises, check your work by using the answer key on page 151. For each right answer, put a check mark (✓) on the line beside the box. For each wrong answer, write the correct answer on the line.*

- *For scoring each exercise, follow the directions below the questions.*

A FINDING THE MAIN IDEA

Look at the three statements below. One expresses the main idea of the story you just read. A good main idea statement answers two questions: it tells *who* or *what* is the subject of the story, and it answers the understood question *does what?* or *is what?* Another statement is *too broad*, it is vague and doesn't tell much about the topic of the story. The third statement is *too narrow*, it tells about only one part of the story.

Match the statements with the three answer choices below by writing the letter of each answer in the box in front of the statement it goes with.

M—Main Idea   B—Too Broad   N—Too Narrow

____ ☐ 1. Science fiction space monsters started to be created in great numbers in the 1950s, when serious space exploration began.

____ ☐ 2. Monsters have always appealed to people's imaginations, and they have been a part of all art forms, from literature to movies.

____ ☐ 3. There have been monster movies almost as long as there have been movies, and the monsters have usually reflected people's fears and imaginings.

____ Score 15 points for a correct *M* answer

____ Score 5 points for each correct *B* or *N* answer

____ TOTAL SCORE: Finding the Main Idea

B RECALLING FACTS

How well do you remember the facts in the story you just read? Put an x in the box in front of the correct answer to each of the multiple-choice questions below.

1. The notion of the "double" is that each individual
   - ___ ☐ a. is mainly evil inside.
   - ___ ☐ b. has both a good and an evil person within.
   - ___ ☐ c. has two evil forces battling within.

2. The German style of horror film, made in the 1930s, used
   - ___ ☐ a. giant insects and oozing blobs of slime.
   - ___ ☐ b. the ideas of atomic energy and space aliens.
   - ___ ☐ c. shadows, mists and strange camera angles.

3. Lon Chaney, Jr. played
   - ___ ☐ a. a werewolf.
   - ___ ☐ b. Frankenstein's monster.
   - ___ ☐ c. Dracula.

4. Atomic monsters and space creatures were the most popular movie monsters of the
   - ___ ☐ a. 1930s.
   - ___ ☐ b. 1950s.
   - ___ ☐ c. 1960s.

5. Godzilla was a
   - ___ ☐ a. giant ape born in an atomic blast.
   - ___ ☐ b. space creature in the film *Buck Rogers in the Twenty-Fifth Century.*
   - ___ ☐ c. a huge dinosaur-like creature with atomic breath.

Score 5 points for each correct answer

___ TOTAL SCORE: Recalling Facts

C MAKING INFERENCES

An inference is a judgment that is made or an idea that is arrived at based on facts or on information that is given. You make an inference when you understand something that is *not* stated directly, but that is *implied,* or suggested by the facts that are given.

Below are five statements that are judgments or ideas that have been arrived at from the facts of the story. Write the letter C in the box in front of each statement that is a correct inference. Write the letter F in front of each faulty inference.

C—Correct Inference   F—Faulty Inference

- ___ ☐ 1. Giant insects never interested moviegoers very much.

- ___ ☐ 2. American horror films would have developed quite differently without the influence of the Germans in the 1930s.

- ___ ☐ 3. People became interested in monsters only after they began appearing in movies.

- ___ ☐ 4. New experiences and discoveries bring new fears, which bring about the creation of new monsters.

- ___ ☐ 5. The earliest space monsters were actually the most frightening.

Score 5 points for each correct answer

___ TOTAL SCORE: Making Inferences

D USING WORDS PRECISELY

Each of the numbered sentences below contains an underlined word or phrase from the story you have just read. Under the sentence are three definitions. One has the *same* meaning as the underlined word or phrase, one has *almost the same* meaning, and one has the *opposite* meaning. Match the definitions with the three answer choices by writing the letter that stands for each answer in the box in front of the definition it goes with.

S—Same   A—Almost the Same   O—Opposite

1. Other monsters, some of them famous and some doomed to obscurity because they were so ridiculous, were created especially for movies.

    ____ ☐ a. the world of fame

    ____ ☐ b. being unknown to most people

    ____ ☐ c. darkness

2. *The Wolf Man* was a taxing movie for Chaney.

    ____ ☐ a. demanding

    ____ ☐ b. easy

    ____ ☐ c. stressful

3. Unfortunately, the rest of the second cycle of horror movies lapsed into imitation, with titles such as *The Ghost of Frankenstein* and *The Mummy's Hand*.

    ____ ☐ a. faded

    ____ ☐ b. sank

    ____ ☐ c. progressed

4. The movies reflected people's fears and imaginings about what might be out there.

    ____ ☐ a. demonstrated

    ____ ☐ b. ignored

    ____ ☐ c. mirrored

5. Space creatures are still with us, but they have largely gone back into the world of fantasy.

    ____ ☐ a. mainly

    ____ ☐ b. in small part

    ____ ☐ c. greatly

____ Score 3 points for each correct *S* answer

____ Score 1 point for each correct *A* or *O* answer

____ TOTAL SCORE: Using Words Precisely

● *Enter the four total scores in the spaces below, and add them together to find your Critical Reading Score. Then record your Critical Reading Score on the graph on page 157.*

_____ Finding the Main Idea
_____ Recalling Facts
_____ Making Inferences
_____ Using Words Precisely
_____ CRITICAL READING SCORE: Unit 8

When Dr. Victor Frankenstein began his experiments to create life, he thought that he would bring a gift to mankind. Instead, he created a grotesque monster. The tragic story of Frankenstein was written nearly one hundred and fifty years ago by eighteen-year-old Mary Shelley. Today, millions of people recognize the wonderfully ugly monster as he is pictured here, portrayed by Boris Karloff, in one of the many successful Frankenstein movies that were made.

Mary Wollstonecraft Shelley wrote the novel Frankenstein, or The Modern Prometheus *as part of a contest with friends to see who could invent the best horror story. Though she later wrote other novels, none achieved the prominence of her imaginative monster story.*

Frankenstein's Monster

The young scientist stood alone in his workroom. It was late at night, and the candle that lighted the room had burned low. In the flickering half-light of that single candle, the man bent over his work table. The only sound in the room was that of rain beating rhythmically against the windowpanes. Suddenly the scientist jumped back in horror. The body that had been lying lifeless on the table was beginning to move. The creature slowly lifted its lids to reveal dull yellow eyes. Its limbs began to twitch, and it started to breathe.

Terrified, the scientist stared at the strange man that he had created. The creature was eight feet tall and had long arms and large hands. His skin was patched and sewn together in many places, and his lips were black. The scientist had hoped that his man would be beautiful. But as he watched him come to life, he saw that his creation was a miserable and disgusting creature.

This is probably the most famous scene in the story of Frankenstein. When that story is mentioned, most people immediately recall the movie versions. But Dr. Frankenstein's dreadful monster was born not in a movie, but in a book. The novel, entitled *Frankenstein,* was written in 1816. In that book, the monster has no name. The young scientist who created him is named Victor Frankenstein. Over the years, people have mistakenly come to refer to the monster as Frankenstein.

The author of *Frankenstein* was eighteen-year-old Mary Wollstonecraft Shelley. Mary Shelley began *Frankenstein* one summer while she and her future husband, the poet Percy Shelley, were vacationing in Switzerland. They, along with Mary's half sister, Jane Clairmont, were visiting with the famous poet Lord Byron. Byron's personal doctor, John Polidori, was also present. On rainy days, the five friends would entertain themselves by reading ghost stories aloud. One night, when they'd again been trapped indoors by a storm, the group was reading a particularly boring German ghost story. To liven things up, Byron proposed a contest. He challenged each of his companions to write a better ghost story than the one they were currently reading.

Only Dr. Polidori and Mary wrote complete stories. Polidori's tale was eventually published under the title *The Vampyre.* The book was highly successful and was later made into an even more successful play. Mary Shelley's story was, of course, *Frankenstein.* It took her eleven months to write.

The tale is that of a young scientist who tried to create life. In one part of the novel, the monster is compared to Adam, the first man. Such a comparison is appropriate, for by giving life to a creature made from assorted body parts, Victor Frankenstein had created a new kind of man. Unfortunately, the result was not what Frankenstein had hoped for. Instead of the beautiful person he had expected to make, he had created a monster that performed a series of horrifying violent deeds.

Shelley's full title for her novel was *Frankenstein, or The Modern Prometheus.* The original Prometheus was a lesser Greek god who gave humans the gift of fire. Zeus, the king of the gods, felt that Prometheus's gift made humans too powerful. Prometheus had gone too far. He had taken too much power unto himself. For that, Zeus decided to punish the little god. He chained Prometheus to the side of a mountain to be tortured by eagles. When Shelley called Frankenstein a modern Prometheus, she was suggesting that like Prometheus the scientist had gone too far. He had done what only God had the right to do—create life. Also like Prometheus, Victor Frankenstein suffered terribly for daring to play God.

The story of Frankenstein and his monster begins in Switzerland. It was there that the scientist received his education. It was also there that he began to devote himself to the mystery of the creation of life. He conducted many experiments, using bodies that he stole from cemeteries. Frankenstein finally learned the secret of life, and found that he was able to bring the spark of life to non-living material.

So the scientist went to work to create a new man. Shutting himself off from his family and friends, he spent endless hours in his laboratory. He emerged only to raid cemeteries for organs and limbs. He worked day and night, wrecking his health. At last he succeeded in bringing the creature to life. But as soon as he had done so, he was filled with regret. He fled in horror from the monster. Then he suffered a nervous breakdown.

What Frankenstein did not take the time to discover was that the monster was a kind and gentle soul. He wanted to be loved and to take part in the world of men. But his hideous form made everyone, even his creator, run from him in fear. In pain and anger then, the creature turned to violence.

After a time, Frankenstein regained his health. But tragedy soon struck. His younger brother was strangled by an unknown murderer. Quickly Victor traveled to the scene of his brother's death. As he stood there in the dark, a flash of lightning cut across the sky. In that eerie light, Victor saw a grotesque figure outlined against the sky. It was his monster. In that brief, terrible moment, Frankenstein knew that it was his creation that had killed his brother.

Victor told no one of his discovery. He did not dare reveal that he had created a monster. Even when an innocent man was hanged as his brother's killer, he maintained his silence. During that period, Victor thought often of ending his own life. But he realized that he was the only one who could save his friends and family from future attacks by the monster.

Then the creature went to Frankenstein. He had learned to speak, and he used his new ability to make a terrible demand. He ordered Victor to create a female companion for him. He warned that if Frankenstein refused, he would begin killing the other members of his family. In the face of that threat, Frankenstein agreed to make a mate for the monster. In return, the creature promised never again to have anything to do with humans.

Dr. Frankenstein created the female monster, as he had promised. But as he finished his work, he was overcome with serious misgivings. What if this male-female pair mated to breed a race of hideous creatures? The monsters could turn out to be enemies of all humankind. To prevent such a tragedy, Frankenstein destroyed the female. When the monster discovered the death of his mate, he swore a terrible revenge, and then vanished.

The monster's revenge was swift. He murdered both Victor's bride and his best friend. In response, Frankenstein pursued the monster all over the world, seeking to destroy it. The chase led him to the frozen wastelands of the North. The monster led him across the treacherous ice of the Arctic Ocean. The creature finally got away when the ice broke apart and separated him from Frankenstein. Victor was carried off on a drifting ice floe. Although the scientist was rescued by a whaling ship, he died soon after.

Borne on his own chunk of floating ice, the monster drifted to the ship that carried his creator's body. There he wept for what he had done. He wept also for what had been done to him—for the hopeless life that he had been given. He vowed that he would punish himself. In so doing, he would also free himself from misery. He said that he would build a funeral pyre and destroy himself by setting himself afire. Then he got back on the chunk of ice and floated away, never to be seen again. ■

If you have been timed while reading this selection, enter your reading time below. Then turn to the Words per Minute table on page 155 and look up your reading speed (words per minute). Enter your reading speed on the graph on page 156.

<table>
<tr><td colspan="2">READING TIME: Unit 9</td></tr>
<tr><td>_____ :</td><td>_____</td></tr>
<tr><td>*Minutes*</td><td>*Seconds*</td></tr>
</table>

How well did you read?

- *Answer the four types of questions that follow. The directions for each type of question tell you how to mark your answers.*

- *When you have finished all four exercises, check your work by using the answer key on page 151. For each right answer, put a check mark (✔) on the line beside the box. For each wrong answer, write the correct answer on the line.*

- *For scoring each exercise, follow the directions below the questions.*

A FINDING THE MAIN IDEA

Look at the three statements below. One expresses the main idea of the story you just read. A good main idea statement answers two questions: it tells *who* or *what* is the subject of the story, and it answers the understood question *does what?* or *is what?* Another statement is *too broad,* it is vague and doesn't tell much about the topic of the story. The third statement is *too narrow,* it tells about only one part of the story.

Match the statements with the three answer choices below by writing the letter of each answer in the box in front of the statement it goes with.

M—Main Idea   **B—Too Broad**   **N—Too Narrow**

_____ ☐ 1. Frankenstein is a chilling monster story that remains popular more than 150 years after it was created.

_____ ☐ 2. Mary Wollstonecraft Shelley wrote the story of Frankenstein in 1816, when she was just eighteen years old, as an entry in a friendly contest.

_____ ☐ 3. Frankenstein originated as a novel in which a horrible and pathetic monster is created by a scientist who wants the power to create life.

_____ Score 15 points for a correct *M* answer
_____ Score 5 points for each correct *B* or *N* answer

_____ TOTAL SCORE: Finding the Main Idea

71

B RECALLING FACTS

How well do you remember the facts in the story you just read? Put an x in the box in front of the correct answer to each of the multiple-choice questions below.

1. In the original title for her novel, Mary Shelley compared Victor Frankenstein to
   ___ ☐ a. a monster.
   ___ ☐ b. Zeus.
   ___ ☐ c. Prometheus.

2. Frankenstein destroyed the female he created because
   ___ ☐ a. he wanted to punish his monster.
   ___ ☐ b. he was afraid that she would breed more monsters.
   ___ ☐ c. she was a hideous creature.

3. Victor Frankenstein died
   ___ ☐ a. on an ice floe in the Arctic.
   ___ ☐ b. in his monster's arms.
   ___ ☐ c. on board a whaling ship.

4. When he had just come to life, Frankenstein's monster was
   ___ ☐ a. ugly but kind and gentle.
   ___ ☐ b. ugly and violent.
   ___ ☐ c. sad and ugly.

5. The first person that the monster killed was Frankenstein's
   ___ ☐ a. friend.
   ___ ☐ b. brother.
   ___ ☐ c. bride.

Score 5 points for each correct answer

___ TOTAL SCORE: Recalling Facts

C MAKING INFERENCES

An inference is a judgment that is made or an idea that is arrived at based on facts or on information that is given. You make an inference when you understand something that is *not* stated directly, but that is *implied,* or suggested by the facts that are given.

Below are five statements that are judgments or ideas that have been arrived at from the facts of the story. Write the letter *C* in the box in front of each statement that is a correct inference. Write the letter *F* in front of each faulty inference.

C—Correct Inference   F—Faulty Inference

___ ☐ 1. Mary Shelley was the most gifted writer of the five friends who vacationed together in 1816.

___ ☐ 2. More movies have been made about Frankenstein's monster than about any other monster.

___ ☐ 3. If Victor Frankenstein had not been horrified by the ugliness of his creation, the monster might not have become violent.

___ ☐ 4. The story of Frankenstein is a modern retelling of a Greek myth.

___ ☐ 5. Mary Shelley was knowledgeable about Greek mythology.

Score 5 points for each correct answer

___ TOTAL SCORE: Making Inferences

D USING WORDS PRECISELY

Each of the numbered sentences below contains an underlined word or phrase from the story you have just read. Under the sentence are three definitions. One has the *same* meaning as the underlined word or phrase, one has *almost the same* meaning, and one has the *opposite* meaning. Match the definitions with the three answer choices by writing the letter that stands for each answer in the box in front of the definition it goes with.

S—Same   **A—Almost the Same**   **O—Opposite**

1. In that eerie light, Victor saw a grotesque figure outlined against the sky.

____ ☐ a. finely built

____ ☐ b. unusual

____ ☐ c. monstrous

2. But as he finished his work, he was overcome with serious misgivings.

____ ☐ a. doubts

____ ☐ b. concerns

____ ☐ c. certainties

3. He emerged only to raid cemeteries for organs and limbs.

____ ☐ a. fled

____ ☐ b. came out

____ ☐ c. stayed inside

4. Even when an innocent man was hanged as his brother's killer, he maintained his silence.

____ ☐ a. gave up

____ ☐ b. kept

____ ☐ c. strengthened

5. Borne on his own chunk of floating ice, the monster drifted to the ship that carried his creator's body.

____ ☐ a. held

____ ☐ b. trapped in place

____ ☐ c. carried

____ Score 3 points for each correct S answer

____ Score 1 point for each correct A or O answer

____ TOTAL SCORE: Using Words Precisely

● *Enter the four total scores in the spaces below, and add them together to find your Critical Reading Score. Then record your Critical Reading Score on the graph on page 157.*

_____ Finding the Main Idea
_____ Recalling Facts
_____ Making Inferences
_____ Using Words Precisely

_____ CRITICAL READING SCORE: Unit 9

In hopes of defeating the Minotaur, a terrible beast half man and half bull, Theseus entered the Labyrinth. Once inside, no one had ever been able to find the way out of that enormous maze. All who entered became a meal for the monster. But Theseus entered armed with an important clue and some good advice. The illustration shown here is an artist's interpretation of Theseus's battle with the Minotaur. In the Greek myth as told in the story you are about to read, however, the Minotaur meets its end in a somewhat different fashion.

The Minotaur

Theseus was the son of Aegeus, king of Athens. But he was born and raised in his mother's home in a city in southern Greece, far from Athens. As a child, he never met his father, for the king returned to Athens before the boy was born. Just before leaving, Aegeus placed a sword and sandals under a large stone and instructed his wife to send their son to Athens when the boy was strong enough to move the stone and remove the objects beneath it. "I will recognize the sword and sandals," Aegeus told his wife, "and I will know that the one who bears them is my son and that he has grown into a tall, strong man."

Over the years, Theseus's mother watched her son grow, until finally she thought the time was right. Then she took him to the stone, and he cast it away with ease. Taking the sword and sandals, the young man set out for his father's kingdom.

When Theseus reached Athens, he was met by Aegeus, who was delighted to see his son at last. The time for joy was short, however, for Theseus had arrived in Athens at the worst possible time. King Minos of the island of Crete was looking for fourteen new victims for the Minotaur.

On Crete, King Minos kept a terrible beast, half man and half bull, called the Minotaur. It lived within an enormous maze called the Labyrinth. The Labyrinth was cleverly constructed, with miles and miles of winding passages, unexpected turnings and dead ends. It was so complex, in fact, that people who were put into it could never find their way out. They simply wandered until the Minotaur found and devoured them. To satisfy the Minotaur's appetite, Minos put seven young men and seven maidens into the maze each year.

The victims were always collected from Athens. Years before, King Minos had sent his only son on a visit to Athens. While the young man was there, King Aegeus sent him on a mission to kill a dangerous bull. He was killed by the bull. In a rage, Minos invaded Athens and declared that he would destroy it unless every year the people sent him seven men and seven maidens to sacrifice to the Minotaur.

When Theseus learned of the situation, he offered himself as one of the victims. Aegeus begged him not to go, but the young man would not listen to his father's entreaties. Theseus told him that he was confident that he could defeat the Minotaur. So when the victims' ship set sail for Crete, Theseus was on board.

They set out with the wind filling the black sail that was customarily used for the ship carrying victims to the Minotaur. Theseus promised his father that when he returned he would replace the black sail with a white one, so that Aegeus would know long before his son set foot in Athens again that he was safe.

When the Athenian ship reached Crete, the fourteen victims were presented to King Minos and his daughter, Ariadne. As soon as Ariadne looked upon the handsome Theseus, she fell deeply in love with him. Ariadne went secretly to Daedalus, who had constructed the Labyrinth, and asked him to show her a way to get out of it. Then she sent for Theseus and told him she would help him escape if he would promise to marry her and take her back to Athens with him. Theseus readily agreed.

In accordance with the clue she had been given, Ariadne secretly gave Theseus a ball of string. She told him to tie it to the gate when he entered the Labyrinth, and to unroll it as he went along. He need only follow it back to find his way out. Then Ariadne told him one other thing. The Minotaur could be slain only if its brain was pierced by one of its own horns.

As Theseus entered the Labyrinth with the other victims, he unwound the ball of string as he had been instructed. He traveled the twisting, turning passageways of the maze until he sensed that he was nearing the center. Then, from up ahead, he heard a stamping of hooves that made the earth tremble. The Minotaur was near.

Theseus advanced slowly around the next few corners. At last the walls of the Labyrinth opened into a wide courtyard with a circular hedge of prickly briars in the center. Theseus listened for some clue to the monster's position, but there was only silence. Theseus sensed that from somewhere behind the briars two evil eyes were watching him.

Suddenly, with a mighty roar, the Minotaur burst from behind the hedge. It charged toward Theseus with its head down and its two great horns flashing in the sunlight. As the beast rushed forward, it appeared that Theseus would surely be impaled on its deadly horns. But the youth was ready for the attack. When the Minotaur was just a few feet from him, Theseus stepped aside, and as the beast flashed by, Theseus grabbed one of its horns in a wrestler's grip. He twisted his body sharply, throwing all his weight to one side. With a crack like a branch being torn from an oak tree in a wind-storm, the horn was wrenched from its socket. The Minotaur bellowed in pain and rage.

Before the monster could collect itself to charge again, Theseus lifted the horn high and thrust it with all his might at the Minotaur's head. The horn shot through the monster's skull and pierced its brain. The Minotaur uttered a terrible cry that was part animal and part human. Then it dropped to the ground, felled by the very weapon that it had used to take so many lives.

Remembering Ariadne's instructions, Theseus then quickly began following the cord back along the passageways through which he had traveled. He easily made his way out of the Labyrinth. Ariadne and the thirteen Athenians were overjoyed at Theseus's success. Together they made their way back to the ship and sailed for Athens.

On the homeward journey, they stopped at the island of Naxos. While the young people were resting, the goddess Athena appeared to Theseus in a dream. She said that Ariadne was destined to wed a god, and that Theseus must not come between the princess and her fate. So Theseus left Ariadne on Naxos and set sail again for Athens.

As the ship neared the coast of Athens, Theseus forgot about the signal he had arranged with his father. He neglected to pull down the black sail and raise the white one. King Aegeus, anxious about his son, had been standing for days on a cliff above the sea, scanning the horizon for the returning ship. When he caught sight of the vessel coming toward him under a black sail, the king was overcome with grief. In his anguish, he threw himself into the sea and was killed. From that day on, the sea was called the Aegean.

When Theseus arrived in Athens, he mourned the death of his father. The people praised him as a hero for killing the Minotaur, and he was made king. ■

If you have been timed while reading this selection, enter your reading time below. Then turn to the Words per Minute table on page 155 and look up your reading speed (words per minute). Enter your reading speed on the graph on page 156.

READING TIME: Unit 10

_____ : _____
Minutes   *Seconds*

How well did you read?

- *Answer the four types of questions that follow. The directions for each type of question tell you how to mark your answers.*

- *When you have finished all four exercises, check your work by using the answer key on page 151. For each right answer, put a check mark (✔) on the line beside the box. For each wrong answer, write the correct answer on the line.*

- *For scoring each exercise, follow the directions below the questions.*

A ⬛ FINDING THE MAIN IDEA

Look at the three statements below. One expresses the main idea of the story you just read. A good main idea statement answers two questions: it tells *who* or *what* is the subject of the story, and it answers the understood question *does what?* or *is what?* Another statement is *too broad*, it is vague and doesn't tell much about the topic of the story. The third statement is *too narrow*, it tells about only one part of the story.

Match the statements with the three answer choices below by writing the letter of each answer in the box in front of the statement it goes with.

M—Main Idea   B—Too Broad   N—Too Narrow

_____ ☐ 1. Theseus marked his path through the Labyrinth by unwinding a ball of string as he walked.

_____ ☐ 2. Against great odds, Theseus destroyed a terrible monster that had been devouring people.

_____ ☐ 3. By destroying the terrible Minotaur, Theseus became a hero in Athens.

_____ Score 15 points for a correct *M* answer

_____ Score 5 points for each correct *B* or *N* answer

_____ TOTAL SCORE: Finding the Main Idea

B RECALLING FACTS

How well do you remember the facts in the story you just read?
Put an x in the box in front of the correct answer to each of the
multiple-choice questions below.

1. When the ship set sail for the island of Crete, it
   was under a
   ____ ☐ a. black sail.
   ____ ☐ b. red sail.
   ____ ☐ c. white sail.

2. Ariadne had obtained the secret to getting out of the
   Labyrinth from
   ____ ☐ a. Daedalus.
   ____ ☐ b. King Aegeus.
   ____ ☐ c. Athena.

3. Theseus found the Minotaur
   ____ ☐ a. hiding behind a hedge of briars.
   ____ ☐ b. peering out of a cave.
   ____ ☐ c. in a narrow passage of the Labyrinth.

4. Theseus used the Minotaur's horn to
   ____ ☐ a. cut off its head.
   ____ ☐ b. stab its heart.
   ____ ☐ c. puncture its head.

5. Athena told Theseus to give up Ariadne so that the
   girl could
   ____ ☐ a. return to her father.
   ____ ☐ b. become her servant.
   ____ ☐ c. marry a god.

Score 5 points for each correct answer

____ TOTAL SCORE: Recalling Facts

C MAKING INFERENCES

An inference is a judgment that is made or an idea that is
arrived at based on facts or on information that is given. You
make an inference when you understand something that is *not*
stated directly, but that is *implied,* or suggested by the facts that
are given.

Below are five statements that are judgments or ideas that
have been arrived at from the facts of the story. Write the letter
C in the box in front of each statement that is a correct inference. Write the letter *F* in front of each faulty inference.

C—Correct Inference   F—Faulty Inference

____ ☐ 1. The Labyrinth covered most of the island
            of Crete.

____ ☐ 2. Theseus was a fearless young man.

____ ☐ 3. Theseus agreed to take Ariadne back to Athens
            with him because he loved her.

____ ☐ 4. Theseus left the black sail up on purpose, because
            he knew that his father would kill himself and he
            would become king.

____ ☐ 5. Ariadne did not know that it was her destiny to
            marry a god.

Score 5 points for each correct answer

____ TOTAL SCORE: Making Inferences

D USING WORDS PRECISELY

Each of the numbered sentences below contains an underlined word or phrase from the story you have just read. Under the sentence are three definitions. One has the *same* meaning as the underlined word or phrase, one has *almost the same* meaning, and one has the *opposite* meaning. Match the definitions with the three answer choices by writing the letter that stands for each answer in the box in front of the definition it goes with.

S—Same   **A—Almost the Same**   **O—Opposite**

1. Aegeus begged him not to go, but the young man would not listen to his father's entreaties.

____ ☐ a. pleadings

____ ☐ b. orders

____ ☐ c. wishes

2. In accordance with the clue she had been given, Ariadne secretly gave Theseus a ball of string.

____ ☐ a. in opposition

____ ☐ b. in agreement

____ ☐ c. in favor

3. Then it dropped to the ground, felled by the very weapon that it had used to take so many lives.

____ ☐ a. knocked over

____ ☐ b. saved

____ ☐ c. cut down

4. She said that Ariadne was destined to wed a god, and that Theseus must not come between the princess and her fate.

____ ☐ a. not meant

____ ☐ b. due to accomplish

____ ☐ c. supposed

5. In his anguish, he threw himself into the sea and was killed.

____ ☐ a. great sorrow

____ ☐ b. unhappiness

____ ☐ c. joy

____ Score 3 points for each correct S answer
____ Score 1 point for each correct A or O answer

____ TOTAL SCORE: Using Words Precisely

● *Enter the four total scores in the spaces below, and add them together to find your Critical Reading Score. Then record your Critical Reading Score on the graph on page 157.*

_____	Finding the Main Idea
_____	Recalling Facts
_____	Making Inferences
_____	Using Words Precisely
_____	CRITICAL READING SCORE: Unit 10

*The Bible story of the giant Goliath who
was killed by a young shepherd named
David is one of the most famous giant
stories of all time. Tales of giants have
existed since ancient times. Did they really
exist at one time? If not, why did so many
people believe in them?*

Giants

Thousands of years ago, people from all parts of the world believed in the existence of giants. Over time, stories of the giants were passed down to new generations. Many of those stories are still with us today. Most people think the tales are ridiculous, of course. But there are those who believe that the stories are true. They believe that in early days a race of giants did roam the earth. Many kinds of evidence are offered to support the idea that giants truly existed.

One source of evidence is the Bible. The Bible contains several stories of giants. Probably the most famous is the one about the Philistine giant, Goliath. According to the Bible, Goliath stood "six cubits and a span," or ten feet nine inches tall. He wore a coat of armor and carried a sword and shield. When a young Hebrew shepherd named David set out to fight the fierce giant, it seemed certain that Goliath would win. David was much smaller than Goliath, and was armed only with a sling—a short leather strap with a string attached to each end, used for throwing stones. With his sling, David could hurl a stone with great speed and accuracy. Even so, he seemed no match for the mighty Goliath.

When Goliath and David confronted each other, the young shepherd picked up a small, smooth stone. Aiming at the one unprotected part of the giant's body, his forehead, David placed the stone in his sling and whirled the simple weapon over his head. He let the stone fly, and it struck Goliath directly on the forehead. As a result of that blow, the Bible says, the giant "fell to his face upon the earth."

Another giant that was legendary in Biblical times was Og, king of Bashan. Og is said to have lived for three thousand years. He supposedly survived the Great Flood of Noah's time by climbing on the roof of the ark. In the daytime, Og waded along beside the ark. At night Noah let him use the ark's roof as a bed. Og scooped fish out of the flood waters for food. He roasted the fish by holding them up to the sun.

According to a Hebrew myth, Og finally died when he quarreled with the ancient Hebrews. In his anger, he picked up a mountain to throw at his enemies. He became so entangled in his burden, however, that Moses was able to kill him. Legend says that the ancient Hebrews then took one of Og's bones and used it to bridge a river.

Giants appear in the myths of almost all cultures. The ancient Greeks believed in a race of giants called the Cyclopes (seye-CLO-peez). A Cyclops was thought to be a huge, primitive creature with one eye, located in the middle of its forehead. Most ancient Greeks were quick to admit that they had never actually seen a living cyclops. But many believed that they had seen the skull of one of the monsters. The skull, which was kept in a special place, was enormous. It had what appeared to be a single eye socket centered in its forehead.

Today most scientists are convinced that the skull did not belong to a cyclops. What the Greeks thought was the skull of a giant one-eyed monster was really the skull of an elephant. The confusion began when someone took an elephant skull from Africa to Greece. There were no elephants in Greece, and the Greeks had no way of knowing about the huge beasts. The elephant skull had a big opening in the center, where the trunk had joined the head. It was logical for the Greeks to assume that the opening in the skull was the socket of a one-eyed giant.

Today people who believe in giants often point to the great pyramids of Egypt as proof that enormous people once lived on earth. The pyramids, and the stone Sphinx that guards them, were built over four thousand years ago. Since heavy construction machinery did not exist in those days, it is hard to imagine how those mammoth structures were erected. Some people argue that mere mortals could not have moved the huge stones into place by hand. They believe that it would have taken giants to complete the immense monuments.

Legends of Native Americans provide another source of stories about giants. Some Native Americans believe that the first human beings on earth were a tribe of gigantic Indians. Those Indians were so large that even buffalo seemed tiny next to them. One giant could easily lift a buffalo, throw it over his shoulder, and carry it back to camp. It is said that even a year-old buffalo calf was so small to those giant humans that they could hang the calves from their belts, the way hunters today might carry rabbits.

According to legend, the giant Indians did as they pleased. They paid no attention to the Great Spirit. Their disregard made the Great Spirit so angry that he decided to punish them. He caused the rivers, lakes and seas to overflow, turning the land to mud. The giants were so heavy that they sank into the wet earth and drowned. Some Native Americans claim that the massive bones of the giants can be seen even today. They are the boulders and rocks of the North American countryside.

Viking myths of ancient Sweden, Norway and Denmark tell of yet another breed of giants. According to the myths, the first living creature was a terrible giant named Ymir. Ymir was slain by Buri, one of the earliest gods. Buri then used Ymir's body to make the earth. The giant's blood formed the seas and lakes. His flesh became the soil. Clouds were made from his brains, and the mountains were formed from his bones. Ymir's hair became the growing things of the earth, and the dome of his skull became the sky.

In addition to explaining the part giants played in the beginning of the world, Viking myths tell of the giants' role in the end of the world. The myths predict that one day giants will enter into a long and terrible struggle with the gods. The fight will lead to chaos. Finally, after three terrible winters in a row, there will come a day of doom in which the entire universe will be destroyed. The seas will boil, earthquakes will rip through the land, and as all the forces of evil are turned loose, the dead will rise from their graves. The newly-risen dead will join the giants and monsters of land and sea in a final battle against the gods. Only four gods and two humans will survive. After the battle, the earth will slowly rise again from beneath the waters. On that fresh green earth the two humans, a man and a woman, will start a new family. Slowly they will rebuild the land and create a new world.

Did giants really exist? If they did, were they the giants of the myths and legends? Well, there have always been some people who have grown far above the normal height and size of other human beings. But there is no physical evidence that there were ever entire races of giants. Some of the myths and legends grew up from people's efforts to explain things—such as the beginning of the earth and the building of the pyramids—for which they had no scientific explanation. Others were born when the huge skeletons of monsters from the past—dinosaurs and other huge, now extinct beasts—were discovered, before there was scientific knowledge of such creatures. So, yes, there have been, and still are, giants of a sort. But the powerful and colorful giants of myth and legend lived mainly in the land of imagination. ■

If you have been timed while reading this selection, enter your reading time below. Then turn to the Words per Minute table on page 155 and look up your reading speed (words per minute). Enter your reading speed on the graph on page 156.

READING TIME: Unit 11
_____ : _____
Minutes   *Seconds*

How well did you read?

- *Answer the four types of questions that follow. The directions for each type of question tell you how to mark your answers.*

- *When you have finished all four exercises, check your work by using the answer key on page 151. For each right answer, put a check mark (✔) on the line beside the box. For each wrong answer, write the correct answer on the line.*

- *For scoring each exercise, follow the directions below the questions.*

A FINDING THE MAIN IDEA

Look at the three statements below. One expresses the main idea of the story you just read. A good main idea statement answers two questions: it tells *who* or *what* is the subject of the story, and it answers the understood question *does what?* or *is what?* Another statement is *too broad*, it is vague and doesn't tell much about the topic of the story. The third statement is *too narrow*, it tells about only one part of the story.

Match the statements with the three answer choices below by writing the letter of each answer in the box in front of the statement it goes with.

M—Main Idea　　**B—Too Broad**　　**N—Too Narrow**

____ ☐ 1. The Bible is the source of some of the most famous giant stories, including the stories of Goliath and of Og, the king of Bashan.

____ ☐ 2. Giants have lived in the myths and legends of almost all the earth's cultures, and most came about as a way of explaining otherwise unexplainable phenomena.

____ ☐ 3. The idea of giants has fascinated people for thousands of years.

____ Score 15 points for a correct *M* answer

____ Score 5 points for each correct *B* or *N* answer

____ TOTAL SCORE: Finding the Main Idea

B RECALLING FACTS

How well do you remember the facts in the story you just read? Put an *x* in the box in front of the correct answer to each of the multiple-choice questions below.

1. Goliath was a
   - ___ ☐ a. Palestinian.
   - ___ ☐ b. Philistine.
   - ___ ☐ c. Philippian.

2. The Biblical giant Og
   - ___ ☐ a. slept on the roof of Noah's ark.
   - ___ ☐ b. killed Moses.
   - ___ ☐ c. was killed by a young shepherd named David.

3. Some Greeks believed that the existence of giants called Cyclopes was proved by what was found to be the
   - ___ ☐ a. skull of a cyclops.
   - ___ ☐ b. rocks and boulders of the countryside.
   - ___ ☐ c. skull of an elephant.

4. According to legend, the giant Indians of North America were punished because they
   - ___ ☐ a. hung buffalo calves from their belts.
   - ___ ☐ b. were so heavy they sank into the mud.
   - ___ ☐ c. ignored the Great Spirit.

5. According to Viking legend, at the time of the final disaster, the dead will rise and do battle with the
   - ___ ☐ a. giants.
   - ___ ☐ b. monsters of land and sea.
   - ___ ☐ c. gods.

Score 5 points for each correct answer

___ TOTAL SCORE: Recalling Facts

C MAKING INFERENCES

An inference is a judgment that is made or an idea that is arrived at based on facts or on information that is given. You make an inference when you understand something that is *not* stated directly, but that is *implied*, or suggested by the facts that are given.

Below are five statements that are judgments or ideas that have been arrived at from the facts of the story. Write the letter *C* in the box in front of each statement that is a correct inference. Write the letter *F* in front of each faulty inference.

C—Correct Inference   F—Faulty Inference

- ___ ☐ 1. It is almost certain that the pyramids were built by a race of giants.
- ___ ☐ 2. Most Greeks still do not know anything about elephants.
- ___ ☐ 3. The Viking myths about giants and the part they will play in the end of the world are taken from the Bible.
- ___ ☐ 4. People believed less and less in giants as scientific knowledge developed.
- ___ ☐ 5. Ymir was the largest of the mythological giants.

Score 5 points for each correct answer

___ TOTAL SCORE: Making Inferences

D USING WORDS PRECISELY

Each of the numbered sentences below contains an underlined word or phrase from the story you have just read. Under the sentence are three definitions. One has the *same* meaning as the underlined word or phrase, one has *almost the same* meaning, and one has the *opposite* meaning. Match the definitions with the three answer choices by writing the letter that stands for each answer in the box in front of the definition it goes with.

S—Same   A—Almost the Same   O—Opposite

1. When Goliath and David <u>confronted</u> each other, the young shepherd picked up a small, smooth stone.

____ ☐ a. faced

____ ☐ b. turned away from

____ ☐ c. met

2. It was <u>logical</u> for the Greeks to assume that the opening in the skull was the socket of a one-eyed, giant human.

____ ☐ a. reasonable

____ ☐ b. thoughtful

____ ☐ c. stupid

3. <u>Mere</u> mortals, they point out, could not have built things as huge as the pyramids or the Sphynx without the use of machinery.

____ ☐ a. pure

____ ☐ b. extraordinary

____ ☐ c. ordinary

4. They paid no attention to the Great Spirit. Their <u>disregard</u> made the Great Spirit so angry that he decided to punish them.

____ ☐ a. neglect

____ ☐ b. attentiveness

____ ☐ c. thoughtlessness

5. Even today, the Indians point out, the <u>massive</u> bones of the giants can be found in the huge boulders and rocks of the North American countryside.

____ ☐ a. small

____ ☐ b. great

____ ☐ c. big and heavy

____ Score 3 points for each correct *S* answer

____ Score 1 point for each correct *A* or *O* answer

____ TOTAL SCORE: Using Words Precisely

● *Enter the four total scores in the spaces below, and add them together to find your Critical Reading Score. Then record your Critical Reading Score on the graph on page 157.*

_____ Finding the Main Idea
_____ Recalling Facts
_____ Making Inferences
_____ Using Words Precisely

_____ CRITICAL READING SCORE: Unit 11

For centuries, the waters of Loch Ness in Scotland have held an intriguing mystery. Thousands of people have reported sighting a huge creature swimming in the lake or moving about on the shore. They describe it as having a long, snakelike neck and a barrel-shaped body. A number of photographs have been taken of the water monster, but some skeptics claim that the objects in the pictures are simply seals or otters or even floating logs. Is there or isn't there a Loch Ness Monster . . . and why is it so hard to find out for sure?

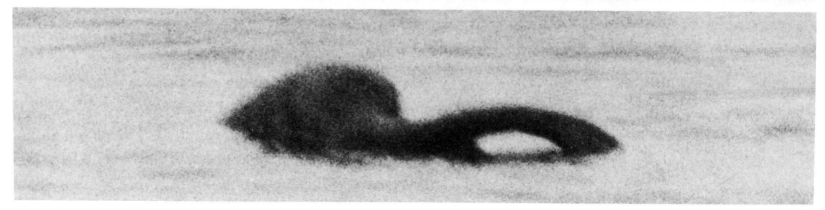

Nessie

The monster said to be living in the waters of Loch Ness in Scotland is not very scary. Nessie, as she is known, does not attack people. She does not destroy property. She does not try to frighten anyone. In fact, she is quite shy. Usually she goes about her own business and avoids humans. For that reason, most people are not afraid of her. But they are curious. They are incredibly curious. People find Nessie so intriguing that thousands of tourists journey to the Highlands of Scotland each year in hopes of seeing her.

Although Nessie now spends most of her time in hiding, she was not always so shy. According to legend, the Loch Ness Monster was once a hostile beast. In 565 A.D., a priest now known as Saint Columba had a very close call with it. He was traveling through Scotland teaching the Christian religion. When he reached the shores of a lake called Loch Ness, he found a funeral in progress. The dead person, he was told, had been killed by the savage bite of a creature living in the lake.

Though the news disturbed him, Columba was determined to cross the lake. He wanted to take his religion to the people living on the other side. Columba asked his servant to wade into the water to get a boat that was nearby. Perhaps the man's splashing disturbed the monster, for suddenly the creature rose from the water. With a menacing roar, Nessie swam straight for the poor servant. Columba rushed forward, his hand raised. Making the sign of the cross in the air, he cried out, "Think not to go further, nor touch thou that man. Quick! Go back!" According to the man who wrote Columba's biography, the monster withdrew as if "dragged by cords."

After her meeting with Saint Columba, Nessie retreated into the depths of Loch Ness. Local folks still caught an occasional glimpse of the monster, but she no longer bothered anybody. In fact she stayed pretty much out of sight until 1933. In that year, a new highway was built next to the lake. During construction, a great deal of dynamite was used to blast through rock. It may have been the noise of the blasting that disturbed Nessie. Or perhaps she was stirred by the boulders that the workmen pushed into the water. In any event, as soon as the highway was opened, Nessie began to appear more often.

Two of the first people to see her at that time were Mr. and Mrs. George Spicer of London. They were traveling on the newly-built highway when Nessie crossed the road ahead of them. It was broad daylight. What was their reaction to the incredible sight? "It was simply horrible," said Mr. Spicer. Mrs. Spicer described Nessie as "a giant snail with a long neck."

Since 1933, around nine thousand sightings have been reported. Nessie has been seen both on land and in the water. Sometimes she appears when the area is almost deserted. But other times she surfaces in full view of many witnesses. Once she showed herself when a bus carrying twenty-seven passengers was passing by. All the people aboard the bus reported that they watched the monster swim for some time. In his book *The Monsters of Loch Ness*, Roy P. Mackal reports 254 detailed eyewitness accounts of sightings of Nessie in the water. He also describes eighteen incidents in which Nessie was seen thrashing around on the shores of Loch Ness.

Many people have tried to photograph Nessie. The most famous picture ever captured of her was taken by a surgeon named H. K. Wilson. Known as the "surgeon's photo," the picture appeared on the front page of a London newspaper, *The Daily Mail*, in 1934. It shows Nessie with a long, thick neck shaped somewhat like an elephant's trunk. Her head is small and flat on top, like the head of a snake. And her huge barrel-shaped body sports a twenty-five-foot tail.

While many people have tried to capture proof of Nessie with a camera (and a number have succeeded in getting pictures much like the surgeon's photo), others have used more complex equipment. Telescopes, binoculars, and movie and television cameras have all been used to look for her. A helicopter and two mini-submarines have hunted her. Sonar has also been used to try to detect her presence. Sonar is a device used to locate underwater objects by bouncing sound waves off them.

Some scientists think that all those efforts have been successful. They say that the sonar results indicate that a large animal is swimming deep in Loch Ness. They also believe that the many photographs and films of Nessie show that she exists. Many pictures show a creature stirring up the water and leaving a trail of waves as it moves along. The scientists argue that such wave patterns could only be created by a huge creature.

Not all scientists, however, are convinced that Nessie is real. Some think that the sonar results proved nothing. Many believe that the creatures in the photographs are simply seals or otters. Others claim that the objects seen in the water are merely sticks or logs.

Part of the reason for all the disagreement is that Nessie is terribly shy. Because she hides from people, it is difficult to observe her. But the confusion is not all her fault. Part of the trouble lies with Loch Ness itself. The lake is very large. It is twenty-four and a half miles long. Some sections are more than 920 feet deep. The water is dark and murky, and its average temperature is only 42 degrees Fahrenheit. The murkiness is caused by peat, which is created by rotting moss and other plants. In Loch Ness the peat is so thick that it is possible to see only to a depth of about ten feet. In addition, the banks of the lake are very steep—almost vertical. Such conditions make photography almost impossible.

While the size of Loch Ness hinders observers, it is ideal for Nessie. Six rivers that flow into Loch Ness bring with them enough fish to feed many monsters. It is estimated that the lake contains 30 million large salmon, plus trout, large pike and char. It also houses tons of fat, juicy eels. Given all that food, chances are that Nessie never goes hungry.

Although the idea of a fish-eating monster may seem a bit strange, there was once a whole group of large creatures that lived on fish. They were dinosaurs called plesiosaurs. They lived in the oceans sixty-five to seventy million years ago. Some people think that Nessie is a descendant of those dinosaurs. It is possible that plesiosaurs got into Loch Ness when it was still part of the Atlantic Ocean. When land later enclosed the lake, the creatures may have gotten trapped there. If Nessie is descended from the plesiosaurs, she may be a member of a whole family of similar creatures living in the waters of Loch Ness.

And speaking of families, Nessie may even have relatives in other parts of the world. Australia has a Nessie-like creature that has been seen in several lakes and rivers. The rivers of Africa, too, contain animals whose descriptions make them sound like first cousins of Nessie. North America also has its Nessie look-alikes. Two lakes in Canada have their own versions of Nessie, and Lake Champlain is home to a monster called Champ. United States monsters also include one that has been spotted in Arkansas's White River. And one in Chesapeake Bay has a name similar to Nessie's. Her name, as you may have guessed, is Chessie. ∎

If you have been timed while reading this selection, enter your reading time below. Then turn to the Words per Minute table on page 155 and look up your reading speed (words per minute). Enter your reading speed on the graph on page 156.

READING TIME: Unit 12

_____ : _____

Minutes   *Seconds*

How well did you read?

- *Answer the four types of questions that follow. The directions for each type of question tell you how to mark your answers.*

- *When you have finished all four exercises, check your work by using the answer key on page 151. For each right answer, put a check mark (✔) on the line beside the box. For each wrong answer, write the correct answer on the line.*

- *For scoring each exercise, follow the directions below the questions.*

A FINDING THE MAIN IDEA

Look at the three statements below. One expresses the main idea of the story you just read. A good main idea statement answers two questions: it tells *who* or *what* is the subject of the story, and it answers the understood question *does what?* or *is what?* Another statement is *too broad,* it is vague and doesn't tell much about the topic of the story. The third statement is *too narrow,* it tells about only one part of the story.

Match the statements with the three answer choices below by writing the letter of each answer in the box in front of the statement it goes with.

M—Main Idea   B—Too Broad   N—Too Narrow

_____ ☐ 1. It is possible that a sea-creature ancestor of Nessie got trapped in Loch Ness when it got closed off from the Atlantic Ocean.

_____ ☐ 2. People have been trying to determine for hundreds of years whether there really is a Loch Ness monster, and there is some evidence for its existence.

_____ ☐ 3. The question of whether or not a monster really exists in Loch Ness has fascinated people for a very long time.

_____ Score 15 points for a correct *M* answer
_____ Score 5 points for each correct *B* or *N* answer

_____ TOTAL SCORE: Finding the Main Idea

B RECALLING FACTS

How well do you remember the facts in the story you just read? Put an x in the box in front of the correct answer to each of the multiple-choice questions below.

1. Saint Columba had gone to the Highlands of Scotland to
   - ☐ a. attend the funeral of a man killed by Nessie.
   - ☐ b. convert the Scots to Christianity.
   - ☐ c. fish in the waters of Loch Ness.

2. The fish in Loch Ness
   - ☐ a. were trapped in it when the lake was cut off from the ocean.
   - ☐ b. come in on the rivers that flow into the loch.
   - ☐ c. have been fished out since the roadway alongside the loch opened in 1933.

3. Mrs. Spicer, who saw Nessie crossing the road in broad daylight, said the monster resembled
   - ☐ a. a snake.
   - ☐ b. the surgeon's photo.
   - ☐ c. a giant snail.

4. The most famous picture of Nessie was taken
   - ☐ a. by a doctor.
   - ☐ b. with sonar.
   - ☐ c. from a mini-submarine.

5. Some scientists think that Nessie may be some sort of
   - ☐ a. brontosaurus.
   - ☐ b. pachyderm.
   - ☐ c. plesiosaur.

Score 5 points for each correct answer

____ TOTAL SCORE: Recalling Facts

C MAKING INFERENCES

An inference is a judgment that is made or an idea that is arrived at based on facts or on information that is given. You make an inference when you understand something that is *not* stated directly, but that is *implied*, or suggested by the facts that are given.

Below are five statements that are judgments or ideas that have been arrived at from the facts of the story. Write the letter C in the box in front of each statement that is a correct inference. Write the letter F in front of each faulty inference.

C—Correct Inference   F—Faulty Inference

- ☐ 1. Saint Columba was made a saint because of the miraculous way in which he handled Nessie.
- ☐ 2. People are still searching for proof of Nessie's existence.
- ☐ 3. Nessie enjoys the attention of all the people who visit Loch Ness to look for her.
- ☐ 4. There may still be creatures living on the earth that no one knows anything about.
- ☐ 5. Nessie herself is thought to have swum into the loch in some past age.

Score 5 points for each correct answer

____ TOTAL SCORE: Making Inferences

90

D USING WORDS PRECISELY

Each of the numbered sentences below contains an underlined word or phrase from the story you have just read. Under the sentence are three definitions. One has the *same* meaning as the underlined word or phrase, one has *almost the same* meaning, and one has the *opposite* meaning. Match the definitions with the three answer choices by writing the letter that stands for each answer in the box in front of the definition it goes with.

S—Same   A—Almost the Same   O—Opposite

1. People find Nessie so intriguing that thousands of tourists journey to the Highlands of Scotland each year in hopes of seeing her.

   _____ ☐ a. amazing

   _____ ☐ b. fascinating

   _____ ☐ c. uninteresting

2. The dead person, he was told, had been killed by the savage bite of a creature living in the lake.

   _____ ☐ a. tender

   _____ ☐ b. vicious

   _____ ☐ c. harsh

3. With a menacing roar, Nessie swam straight for the poor servant.

   _____ ☐ a. reassuring

   _____ ☐ b. disturbing

   _____ ☐ c. threatening

4. After her meeting with Saint Columba, Nessie retreated into the depths of Loch Ness.

   _____ ☐ a. went back

   _____ ☐ b. advanced for the first time

   _____ ☐ c. escaped

5. While the size of Loch Ness hinders observers, it is ideal for Nessie.

   _____ ☐ a. helps

   _____ ☐ b. makes things difficult for

   _____ ☐ c. gets in the way of

_____ Score 3 points for each correct S answer

_____ Score 1 point for each correct A or O answer

_____ TOTAL SCORE: Using Words Precisely

• *Enter the four total scores in the spaces below, and add them together to find your Critical Reading Score. Then record your Critical Reading Score on the graph on page 157.*

_____	Finding the Main Idea
_____	Recalling Facts
_____	Making Inferences
_____	Using Words Precisely
_____	CRITICAL READING SCORE: Unit 12

The head of a lion, the body of a goat, and a snake for a tail. Because of a lie told against him, young Bellerophon was forced to face this monstrous beast. Were his strength and cunning a match for the creature's special powers? He had no choice but to find out.

The Chimera

One of the myths of ancient Greece tells of a she-monster called the Chimera (keye-MIHR-ah), which terrorized the kingdom of Lycia. The Chimera had a lion's head, and from its mouth it breathed fire. Its body was like that of a goat, making it swift and agile. The beast could twist and dodge the most carefully aimed arrows. And the Chimera's tail was a serpent that spit deadly venom. Lycia's strongest and bravest men had tried to rid the kingdom of the terrible creature, but all had failed in their attempts.

One day the king of Lycia received a visitor—a young man named Bellerophon. Bellerophon had traveled from the distant kingdom of Argos. His own king, Proetus (pro-EED-us), had sent him with a message for the king of Lycia. Bellerophon believed that the king would be glad to get the message, for Proetus was married to the king's daughter.

After presenting the letter to the king, Bellerophon waited quietly. Although the young messenger hadn't read the letter, he thought he could guess its contents. He was sure the letter told of his bravery and courage. He was right about that. The letter did state that Bellerophon was a very brave man. But what the unsuspecting young man didn't know was that the letter also requested that the king of Lycia put him to death.

Proetus wrote that Bellerophon had seduced his wife, Lycia's daughter. "To avenge the woman who is my wife and your daughter, you must kill the messenger who brings you this letter," wrote Proetus.

As the king read the letter, he realized that he was in a difficult spot. On the one hand, he should do what Proetus asked. After all, he wanted to defend his daughter's honor and grant his son-in-law's request. But at the same time, he was bound to protect Bellerophon. According to the ancient law of the land, it was a host's duty to protect the lives of his guests. As long as Bellerophon was in the palace, he was the king's guest. So the king was faced with a dilemma. He wasn't sure whether he should kill Bellerophon or offer him protection.

Meanwhile, Bellerophon continued to stand innocently before the throne. He had no reason to suspect that he was in danger. He had not read Proetus's letter. He had no way of knowing that the letter accused him of having an affair with Proetus's wife. In fact, Bellerophon had not tried to win the queen's affections. The truth was just the reverse. The queen had fallen in love with Bellerophon. When he found out, he chose to avoid her. Bellerophon's rejection so angered her that she went to her husband and lied to get Bellerophon in trouble.

The Lycian king studied the message from Proetus. Then he looked at the fine, strong young man standing before him. It seemed to the king that there was no solution to his dilemma. Then in a flash the answer presented itself to him. His problem was solved! He would ask Bellerophon to slay the Chimera!

If Bellerophon was really as brave as the first part of the letter said, the king knew that he would be willing to face the monster. If he succeeded in killing it, the kingdom would be free of the terrible beast. If, on the other hand, he failed, the Chimera would surely kill him. Either way, the king would win. He would either be rid of the monster or he would be able to tell Proetus that his messenger was dead.

"Not far from here," the king told Bellerophon, "is a monster called the Chimera. It has the head of a lion, the body of a goat and a snake for its tail. It must be destroyed, but none of my people will face it. Now if you are as brave a man as this letter says . . ."

Although the king left his sentence unfinished, his meaning was clear. Bellerophon realized that he had to fight the Chimera or be branded a coward. Without a moment's hesitation, Bellerophon accepted the king's challenge.

Bellerophon believed that he could fight and win out over any monster. But he did not know all the facts about the Chimera. The king had not told him how many soldiers had died trying to slay the beast. Bellerophon did not know about the Chimera's flaming breath, which prevented anyone from getting close with hand weapons. He did not know of the monster's quickness or of the deadly bite of its snake tail, which had been the undoing of the best warriors of Lycia. The Chimera was the fiercest creature alive.

Before Bellerophon set out on his task, he sought the advice of a soothsayer. The soothsayer told the youth that his only hope of slaying the monster depended on the winged horse Pegasus. Only if Bellerophon were mounted on Pegasus's back could he possibly succeed. The wings of the magnificent white stallion could carry Bellerophon beyond the reach of the Chimera's fiery breath and deadly tail. But, the soothsayer warned, Pegasus lived wild and free. Bellerophon would have to catch him and train him before he could ride him.

That night the goddess Athena appeared before Bellerophon. She gave him a golden bridle. "Slip this bridle over the head of Pegasus," she told Bellerophon, "and he will let you get on his back and ride him."

When Bellerophon found Pegasus, the stallion was drinking at a spring. Quietly Bellerophon sneaked up close to him. Then in one quick movement he slipped the golden bridle over the horse's head. Pegasus began to snort and stamp his feet furiously, but Bellerophon managed to hold on to him until he calmed down. As soon as Pegasus accepted his loss of freedom, Bellerophon mounted him. Then horse and rider flew off into the sky together.

Beating his mighty wings, Pegasus carried Bellerophon to a flat patch of ground high in the hills. Gazing into the valley below, Bellerophon caught sight of the Chimera's hideous shape. He directed Pegasus to take off again and commanded him to fly near to the beast. As they flew over the Chimera, Bellerophon shot arrow after arrow into her body. Although the arrows weakened the monster, they could not kill her.

Finally Bellerophon pulled out his spear. He had tied a large piece of lead to its tip. When the Chimera opened her great jaws, Bellerophon thrust the spear down her throat. Outraged, the Chimera began shooting flames from her mouth. The monster's fiery breath could not quite reach the winged horse and rider, but the great heat melted the lead on the tip of the spear. The molten lead trickled down the beast's throat, causing the Chimera to die a horribly painful death.

After Bellerophon had destroyed the Chimera, he returned to the king. The king then made Bellerophon perform some other dangerous tasks before admitting that he must, indeed, be a good and worthy man. He decided that Bellerophon could not be guilty of the crime that Proetus had accused him of. He then told the youth what was in the letter. After the king heard Bellerophon's explanation, he arranged for the youth to meet his second daughter. The two fell in love and were married, and there was great celebration throughout the land. ■

If you have been timed while reading this selection, enter your reading time below. Then turn to the Words per Minute table on page 155 and look up your reading speed (words per minute). Enter your reading speed on the graph on page 156.

READING TIME: Unit 13

_____ : _____
Minutes　　*Seconds*

How well did you read?

- *Answer the four types of questions that follow. The directions for each type of question tell you how to mark your answers.*

- *When you have finished all four exercises, check your work by using the answer key on page 151. For each right answer, put a check mark (✔) on the line beside the box. For each wrong answer, write the correct answer on the line.*

- *For scoring each exercise, follow the directions below the questions.*

A FINDING THE MAIN IDEA

Look at the three statements below. One expresses the main idea of the story you just read. A good main idea statement answers two questions: it tells *who* or *what* is the subject of the story, and it answers the understood question *does what?* or *is what?* Another statement is *too broad*, it is vague and doesn't tell much about the topic of the story. The third statement is *too narrow*, it tells about only one part of the story.

Match the statements with the three answer choices below by writing the letter of each answer in the box in front of the statement it goes with.

M—Main Idea   B—Too Broad   N—Too Narrow

_____ ☐ 1. Proetus, the king of Argos, sent Bellerophon to deliver a letter to the king of Lycia, and the message asked the king to have Bellerophon killed.

_____ ☐ 2. With the help of Pegasus, Bellerophon bravely faced and killed the terrible Chimera, thereby winning the friendship of the king of Lycia.

_____ ☐ 3. Bellerophon was a strong, brave Greek youth who tamed the winged horse, Pegasus, and conquered terrible beasts in the Greek myths.

_____ Score 15 points for a correct *M* answer
_____ Score 5 points for each correct *B* or *N* answer

_____ TOTAL SCORE: Finding the Main Idea

B RECALLING FACTS

How well do you remember the facts in the story you just read?
Put an *x* in the box in front of the correct answer to each of the
multiple-choice questions below.

1. When he delivered the message to the king of Lycia,
   Bellerophon was
   - ____ ☐ a. suspicious but unafraid.
   - ____ ☐ b. unsuspicious and unafraid.
   - ____ ☐ c. suspicious and afraid.

2. The queen who accused Bellerophon was the wife of
   - ____ ☐ a. Proetus.
   - ____ ☐ b. the king of Lycia.
   - ____ ☐ c. a Greek god.

3. Bellerophon captured Pegasus
   - ____ ☐ a. by throwing a rope around his neck.
   - ____ ☐ b. with the help of a soothsayer.
   - ____ ☐ c. with a golden bridle.

4. The Chimera was a combination of
   - ____ ☐ a. goat, dragon, and snake.
   - ____ ☐ b. lion, goat, and snake.
   - ____ ☐ c. goat, tiger, and snake.

5. The Chimera was finally killed by
   - ____ ☐ a. the thrust of a spear.
   - ____ ☐ b. many arrows.
   - ____ ☐ c. fiery-hot melted lead.

Score 5 points for each correct answer

____ TOTAL SCORE: Recalling Facts

C MAKING INFERENCES

An inference is a judgment that is made or an idea that is
arrived at based on facts or on information that is given. You
make an inference when you understand something that is *not*
stated directly, but that is *implied,* or suggested by the facts that
are given.

Below are five statements that are judgments or ideas that
have been arrived at from the facts of the story. Write the letter
C in the box in front of each statement that is a correct inference. Write the letter *F* in front of each faulty inference.

C—Correct Inference   F—Faulty Inference

- ____ ☐ 1. Proetus's wife later regretted having lied to her
  husband about Bellerophon.

- ____ ☐ 2. Bellerophon was well-liked by the gods.

- ____ ☐ 3. Pegasus could not be harmed by the Chimera's
  fiery breath.

- ____ ☐ 4. Bellerophon was not afraid of anything.

- ____ ☐ 5. The other dangerous tasks that the king had
  Bellerophon perform all involved killing
  monsters.

Score 5 points for each correct answer

____ TOTAL SCORE: Making Inferences

D USING WORDS PRECISELY

Each of the numbered sentences below contains an underlined word or phrase from the story you have just read. Under the sentence are three definitions. One has the *same* meaning as the underlined word or phrase, one has *almost the same* meaning, and one has the *opposite* meaning. Match the definitions with the three answer choices by writing the letter that stands for each answer in the box in front of the definition it goes with.

S—Same   A—Almost the Same   O—Opposite

1. Its body was like that of a goat, making it swift and agile.

   ____ ☐ a. moving quickly and easily

   ____ ☐ b. slow and clumsy

   ____ ☐ c. graceful

2. The letter did state that Bellerophon was a very brave man.

   ____ ☐ a. deny

   ____ ☐ b. emphasize

   ____ ☐ c. say

3. But at the same time, he was bound to protect Bellerophon.

   ____ ☐ a. determined

   ____ ☐ b. obliged

   ____ ☐ c. not required

4. Bellerophon's rejection so angered her that she went to her husband and lied to get Bellerophon in trouble.

   ____ ☐ a. refusal

   ____ ☐ b. resistance

   ____ ☐ c. acceptance

5. It seemed to the king that there was no solution to his dilemma.

   ____ ☐ a. solution

   ____ ☐ b. difficulty

   ____ ☐ c. problem

____ Score 3 points for each correct *S* answer

____ Score 1 point for each correct *A* or *O* answer

____ TOTAL SCORE: Using Words Precisely

● *Enter the four total scores in the spaces below, and add them together to find your Critical Reading Score. Then record your Critical Reading Score on the graph on page 157.*

_____ Finding the Main Idea
_____ Recalling Facts
_____ Making Inferences
_____ Using Words Precisely

_____ CRITICAL READING SCORE: Unit 13

Lovely sea creatures half woman and half fish. Fierce, deadly snakes with crowns on their heads. A bird that lived for five hundred years, then burned itself to death and came to life again from its own ashes. A flying beast part eagle and part lion. Such creatures never really existed, of course. But for a very long time, people believed that they did.

Creatures of the Imagination

What a remarkable zoo we would have if we could collect the many strange beasts that lived in the myths and legends of peoples of times past. It would be a mysterious and magical place. How did people come to believe in creatures that didn't exist? The reasons are as varied as the creatures themselves.

Christopher Columbus reported that on one of his trips to the Americas he saw three strange figures rise from the sea. He identified the creatures as mermaids. Columbus didn't know it, but he was not the first sailor to see mermaids in the waters near the New World. Five centuries earlier, a Viking seaman wrote of a similar sight. The Vikings saw a tall creature with the head and upper body of a slender woman rise from the sea. Reportedly, the same mermaid appeared several times during the voyage, always shortly before the arrival of a storm. The Vikings decided that she was warning them of the approach of storms. Later, when Henry Hudson explored the New World, he also reported seeing mermaids.

These men were all experienced sailors. They were known as reliable and level-headed people. How could seasoned mariners come to believe in such imaginary creatures as mermaids? Recent scientific studies suggest that the mariners of old were not making up stories. They really did see creatures that looked like mermaids. Scientific studies have shown that under certain conditions of weather and temperature the surface of the sea can cause optical illusions. Such illusions could make a stumpy walrus or a sea cow a mile away appear to be a slender mermaid. And, the scientists add, the weather conditions that produce such optical illusions are present only in the calm period before a storm. So the Viking tale of the mermaid who rose from the sea to give storm warnings makes sense.

The basis for the stories of griffins is a little less clear. The griffin had the head, forepart and wings of an eagle, and the body, hind legs and tail of a lion. The creatures can be found in the myths of Egypt, Persia and ancient Greece. It even makes an appearance in *Alice's Adventures in Wonderland*. Europeans living in the Middle Ages were also familiar with griffins. In fact, the Europeans had a terrible fear of griffins. They believed that they often ate horses and sometimes even devoured people.

Although griffins never existed, some scientists think that they may have been based on real birds. The idea is that the beasts that people once called griffins were actually large vultures called lammergeiers.

The lammergeier is a huge bird. With its four-foot body and ten-foot wingspan, it might well have seemed as big as a lion when it flew overhead. And the vulture's beard must have looked very much like a lion's mane to people staring up at the bird. There is one final bit of evidence for this link between griffins and lammergeiers. Lammergeiers live in the areas in which the legend of griffins flourished.

During the Middle Ages, griffins' claws were big sellers in the European market. The claws did not really come from griffins, of course. They were fakes, sold to gullible people. In fact, they were not really claws at all. Parts of two different animals that have been extinct for thousands of years were sold as griffin claws. They were the tusks of woolly mammoths and the horns of woolly rhinoceroses.

One of the most mystical creatures from ancient myths is the bird known as the phoenix. It was said to be as large as an eagle, and its feathers were brilliant gold and scarlet. Only one phoenix, a male, lived at a time. It had a lifespan of about five hundred years. In Egypt, the phoenix was associated with sun worship. As its lifecycle drew to a close, the phoenix would build a nest of sweet boughs and spices. It would then set the nest on fire and enter the flames to die. From the ashes would spring a new phoenix. It would gather its father's ashes and carry them to the altar of the Egyptian sun god, Re. The connection between the sun and the phoenix is easy to see. The sun sets in its flames each evening, and rises again each morning. The phoenix has also long been a symbol of rebirth—of life after death. In its continual resurrection, the bird is immortal.

One of the most dangerous of all mythical beasts was the basilisk. This animal was known to ancient populations as the king of snakes. Old drawings show the basilisk as a serpent with a crown on its head. In some pictures it is also shown with wings. The mere glance of a basilisk was reputed to be enough to kill its enemy. Eye contact with the serpent was so deadly that the beast could even kill itself if it happened to catch sight of its own reflection. The basilisk also had poisonous breath, and touching any part of its body caused instant death.

People in the Middle Ages often blamed mysterious deaths on the basilisk. Hunts would be organized to track down the deadly beast. People brave enough to go after the serpent carried mirrors. They hoped to avoid death by looking only at the basilisk's reflection, rather than directly at the beast. And if the hunters were lucky enough, the basilisk might glimpse itself in the mirror and be killed by its own deadly gaze.

Descriptions of the basilisk sound far-fetched, but there is a real serpent that has some similarities to it. It is the Indian cobra. The cobra's breath may not be poisonous, but the snake is capable of spitting its venom as far as ten feet. If the venom lands in a person's eyes, the victim can be blinded. It is not hard to imagine how people of old may have thought of the cobra's venom as deadly breath. The appearance of the cobra also roughly matches the drawings of the basilisk. The cobra's hood resembles the small wings of the basilisk.

The stories about basilisks state that the serpent could be killed by a kind of weasel. Perhaps this was a reference to the mongoose of India, a small cousin of the weasel. The mongoose, which is incredibly quick, almost always succeeds in avoiding the cobra's deadly fangs. The mongoose grabs the snake by the back of its neck and bites through its spinal cord, killing it instantly.

All these strange creatures grew from some reasonable basis, considering that at the times when people believed in them, there was little scientific explanation for many of the earth's natural creatures and phenomena. We know now that mermaids, the phoenix, basilisks and griffins don't really exist. But in our literature and art, and in our imaginations, they have given us a rich and magnificent zoo. ■

If you have been timed while reading this selection, enter your reading time below. Then turn to the Words per Minute table on page 155 and look up your reading speed (words per minute). Enter your reading speed on the graph on page 156.

READING TIME: Unit 14

_____ : _____

Minutes   *Seconds*

How well did you read?

- *Answer the four types of questions that follow. The directions for each type of question tell you how to mark your answers.*

- *When you have finished all four exercises, check your work by using the answer key on page 151. For each right answer, put a check mark (✔) on the line beside the box. For each wrong answer, write the correct answer on the line.*

- *For scoring each exercise, follow the directions below the questions.*

A FINDING THE MAIN IDEA

Look at the three statements below. One expresses the main idea of the story you just read. A good main idea statement answers two questions: it tells *who* or *what* is the subject of the story, and it answers the understood question *does what?* or *is what?* Another statement is *too broad,* it is vague and doesn't tell much about the topic of the story. The third statement is *too narrow,* it tells about only one part of the story.

Match the statements with the three answer choices below by writing the letter of each answer in the box in front of the statement it goes with.

M—Main Idea   B—Too Broad   N—Too Narrow

_____ ☐ 1. The wondrous mythical and legendary beasts of old grew up from people's imaginations and their lack of knowledge of some of the earth's real creatures.

_____ ☐ 2. The descriptions of some of the fabulous legendary beasts of old sound a lot like some real animals.

_____ ☐ 3. For thousands of years, people all over the world believed in the existence of incredible creatures.

_____ Score 15 points for a correct *M* answer

_____ Score 5 points for each correct *B* or *N* answer

_____ TOTAL SCORE: Finding the Main Idea

B RECALLING FACTS

How well do you remember the facts in the story you just read?
Put an x in the box in front of the correct answer to each of the
multiple-choice questions below.

1. Columbus and his crew claimed to have seen
   ____ ☐ a. griffins.
   ____ ☐ b. mermaids.
   ____ ☐ c. a basilisk.

2. A griffin is
   ____ ☐ a. part eagle and part lion.
   ____ ☐ b. part bull and part man.
   ____ ☐ c. part bird and part horse.

3. The lammergeier is a
   ____ ☐ a. type of griffin.
   ____ ☐ b. mythological bird.
   ____ ☐ c. huge vulture.

4. Each phoenix was said to live for
   ____ ☐ a. a thousand years.
   ____ ☐ b. five hundred years.
   ____ ☐ c. five thousand years.

5. The mythical basilisk is much like the real
   ____ ☐ a. lammergeier.
   ____ ☐ b. python.
   ____ ☐ c. cobra.

Score 5 points for each correct answer

____ TOTAL SCORE: Recalling Facts

C MAKING INFERENCES

An inference is a judgment that is made or an idea that is
arrived at based on facts or on information that is given. You
make an inference when you understand something that is *not*
stated directly, but that is *implied*, or suggested by the facts that
are given.

Below are five statements that are judgments or ideas that
have been arrived at from the facts of the story. Write the letter
C in the box in front of each statement that is a correct inference. Write the letter *F* in front of each faulty inference.

C—Correct Inference   F—Faulty Inference

____ ☐ 1. The optical illusion that caused Columbus and
          the Vikings to "see" mermaids can occur only in
          warm weather.

____ ☐ 2. Lammergeiers are now extinct.

____ ☐ 3. If people believed that lammergeiers were griffins,
          they must never have seen the birds up close.

____ ☐ 4. The people of the Middle Ages made up
          frightening beasts to account for things they did
          not understand.

____ ☐ 5. Touching the skin of the cobra causes instant
          death.

Score 5 points for each correct answer

____ TOTAL SCORE: Making Inferences

D USING WORDS PRECISELY

Each of the numbered sentences below contains an underlined word or phrase from the story you have just read. Under the sentence are three definitions. One has the *same* meaning as the underlined word or phrase, one has *almost the same* meaning, and one has the *opposite* meaning. Match the definitions with the three answer choices by writing the letter that stands for each answer in the box in front of the definition it goes with.

S—Same   A—Almost the Same   O—Opposite

1. How could <u>seasoned</u> mariners come to believe in such imaginary creatures as mermaids?

____ ☐ a. immature

____ ☐ b. skilled

____ ☐ c. experienced

2. Such <u>illusions</u> could make a stumpy walrus or a sea cow a mile away appear to be a slender mermaid.

____ ☐ a. tricks of eyesight

____ ☐ b. accurate appearances

____ ☐ c. dreamy visions

3. In its continual <u>resurrection</u>, the bird is immortal.

____ ☐ a. death

____ ☐ b. coming to life again

____ ☐ c. rising

4. The mere glance of a basilisk was <u>reputed</u> to be enough to kill its enemy.

____ ☐ a. widely doubted

____ ☐ b. thought

____ ☐ c. popularly believed

5. The appearance of a cobra also <u>roughly</u> matches the drawings of the basilisk.

____ ☐ a. somewhat

____ ☐ b. approximately

____ ☐ c. exactly

____ Score 3 points for each correct S answer

____ Score 1 point for each correct A or O answer

____ TOTAL SCORE: Using Words Precisely

● *Enter the four total scores in the spaces below, and add them together to find your Critical Reading Score. Then record your Critical Reading Score on the graph on page 157.*

_____	Finding the Main Idea
_____	Recalling Facts
_____	Making Inferences
_____	Using Words Precisely
_____	CRITICAL READING SCORE: Unit 14

GROUP THREE

Dripping with slime, the hideous Grendel made nightly raids on local villages, tearing helpless victims to shreds with his daggerlike claws and carrying their bodies back to his swamp to be devoured. Even the king's mighty Viking warriors could do nothing to stop the terrible beast. When Beowulf stepped in to try to put a stop to the slaughter, however, Grendel found that he had met his match.

Grendel

Old King Hrothgar should have been a happy man. He and his Viking warriors were the terrors of the European seas. When his brave men attacked a coastal city or a sailing ship, they were almost always victorious. Their robbings and lootings had made them rich, so when they weren't off fighting, Hrothgar and his men lived in splendor in Denmark. They surrounded themselves with plush furs and brilliant ornaments of gold. In the evenings they gathered in the king's great drinking hall to eat, drink and sing songs. Those celebrations usually ended with everyone collapsing into a long, contented sleep.

Despite all the merrymaking, however, King Hrothgar was deeply troubled. For twelve years, a dark and horrifying creature had been terrorizing Hrothgar's kingdom. The creature, whose name was Grendel, was a monster of human shape but of superhuman size and strength. Each night, the beast dragged himself out of the swamp where he lived and attacked the local villagers. Often when Hrothgar's warriors awoke from their sleep, they found the doors of the drinking hall bashed in and several of their companions missing. The king ordered the doors strengthened with iron bands, but it did no good. Grendel's murderous raids continued.

Finally, in desperation, the Vikings decided to lay a trap for the monster. One night, a group of warriors stationed themselves as guards outside the king's drinking hall. They intended to hide in wait for Grendel and then attack and kill the evil beast. A second band of warriors waited inside the hall, just in case the monster succeeded in getting past the first group.

The Vikings hadn't been lying in wait for long when they spied a huge and fearsome creature approaching. They knew immediately that it was Grendel. Although the creature was stooped over, they could see that he was far taller than any ordinary man. As he came closer, they could see his green, horny skin. It was as tough as armor and could not be penetrated by even the sharpest sword. The men could also see Grendel's long, sharp teeth, which were curved like the tusks of a wild boar. The monster's hands ended in iron nails sharper than daggers. By Grendel's side hung an enormous bag, which he used to carry his victims back to the swamp where he could devour them one by one. But the most horrible of all the demon's features was his hideous face. It was a swollen purple mass with eyes that regarded the world with pure hatred.

When the monster was almost upon them, the Vikings outside the hall fell on him with their swords and spears. But Grendel's thick hide made their weapons useless. With a simple shrug of his powerful shoulders and a sweep of a huge arm, he threw off his attackers. Then he stormed to the door of the hall and blasted it open with a single blow. The Danes waiting inside were no more successful than their companions had been. None of their weapons made the slightest impact on the monster. As the men fought in vain, Grendel's iron claws slashed through their shields and armor. Soon many men had been killed or maimed. The remaining warriors could only watch in horror as the monster headed back toward his swamp, carrying several dead Vikings with him.

At about that time, tales of Grendel's gruesome deeds reached Sweden, where Prince Beowulf lived. Beowulf decided to go to the aid of King Hrothgar. He called together fourteen of his bravest warriors and set sail with them for Denmark. When they reached King Hrothgar's kingdom, they received a warm welcome. The king escorted them to his drinking hall, where he lit a fire in the great fireplace and set before them a feast of food and drink. During the feast, minstrels sang songs about the Viking heroes and their great deeds. Beowulf and his men enjoyed the drinking and boasting. Soon, however, Beowulf announced that it was time for the party to end. King Hrothgar and his people were asked to leave the hall, for Beowulf and his men had to prepare for their meeting with Grendel.

Beowulf's comrades lay down on the benches in the hall to await the arrival of the monster. They remained clothed in their heavy armor, in anticipation of a great struggle. Only Beowulf removed his shining coat of armor with its hundreds of interlocking steel rings. He unbuckled his sword and removed his helmet, saying to his men, "I will strive against this fiend weaponless. I will wrestle him with no armor, since he wears none. I will conquer, if I win, by my hand-grip alone."

Then Beowulf lay down next to his men. The fire in the fireplace provided the only light in the hall. Its flames cast strange shadows around the room. The men watched the shadows silently, waiting for the creature from the swamp. Suddenly there was a great crash. The massive wood and iron door shattered, and in burst the giant figure of Grendel. Before any of the warriors could move, Grendel's hand shot out toward one of Beowulf's men. The man screamed just once before his voice was cut off by a tearing sound. Almost instantly, Grendel had killed the man.

Then Grendel spotted Beowulf. The two sprang at each other in the same instant. Beowulf's hand reached out, caught one of the demon's hairy wrists, and hung fast. Grendel's iron claws reached for Beowulf's throat, but the prince moved more quickly than the monster. Giving the arm a fearful twist, Beowulf hurled Grendel to the floor. With one hand still holding firmly to the creature's wrist, Beowulf then leaped onto his back. The beast rolled and writhed on the floor in an effort to break free from the prince's grasp, but Beowulf hung on.

As the two struggled, they rolled closer and closer to the fireplace. Suddenly Grendel rolled right into the fire and hit his cheek against the burning coals. Shrieking in pain, he shook Beowulf from his shoulders. But even as the prince fell, he kept his grip on the monster's arm. At that point, Grendel wanted only to run back to his swamp. The burn on his face was agonizing, and he was in great pain from having his arm twisted around. He ran toward the doorway of the hall, dragging Beowulf with him.

As the monster struggled to get out the door, Beowulf placed one foot on either side of the door's inner frame. Then he gave Grendel's arm one last, mighty twist. There was a loud snap and an even louder bellow of pain. The monster's arm pulled out of its socket. Grendel fled screaming to his swamp, where he sank to the bottom and died. Back in the hall, Beowulf stood exhausted, still holding the monster's severed arm.

The next night, King Hrothgar held the most wonderful feast ever, in honor of Prince Beowulf. He gave Beowulf and his companions gifts of gold, jewels, horses and armor, and he ordered his minstrels to write song-poems about Beowulf's heroic fight with Grendel.

The story of Beowulf and Grendel is itself part of a long heroic poem entitled *Beowulf*. Composed between the years 700 and 750, it is the oldest epic, or song-poem, in the English language. It is also the greatest piece of Old English literature. ∎

If you have been timed while reading this selection, enter your reading time below. Then turn to the Words per Minute table on page 155 and look up your reading speed (words per minute). Enter your reading speed on the graph on page 156.

READING TIME: Unit 15

_____ : _____
Minutes   *Seconds*

How well did you read?

- *Answer the four types of questions that follow. The directions for each type of question tell you how to mark your answers.*

- *When you have finished all four exercises, check your work by using the answer key on page 152. For each right answer, put a check mark (✔) on the line beside the box. For each wrong answer, write the correct answer on the line.*

- *For scoring each exercise, follow the directions below the questions.*

A FINDING THE MAIN IDEA

Look at the three statements below. One expresses the main idea of the story you just read. A good main idea statement answers two questions: it tells *who* or *what* is the subject of the story, and it answers the understood question *does what?* or *is what?* Another statement is *too broad,* it is vague and doesn't tell much about the topic of the story. The third statement is *too narrow,* it tells about only one part of the story.

Match the statements with the three answer choices below by writing the letter of each answer in the box in front of the statement it goes with.

M—Main Idea   B—Too Broad   N—Too Narrow

_____ ☐ 1. As told in an old Scandinavian legend, the Swedish prince Beowulf helped the Danish Vikings defeat a terrible monster.

_____ ☐ 2. Beowulf killed the fearsome swamp monster Grendel by twisting his arm off.

_____ ☐ 3. Beowulf killed the swamp monster Grendel in the epic poem *Beowulf,* the oldest piece of English literature.

_____ Score 15 points for a correct *M* answer
_____ Score 5 points for each correct *B* or *N* answer

_____ TOTAL SCORE: Finding the Main Idea

B RECALLING FACTS

How well do you remember the facts in the story you just read?
Put an x in the box in front of the correct answer to each of the
multiple-choice questions below.

1. The first thing King Hrothgar did to try to prevent
   Grendel from raiding his hall was
   - ☐ a. lay a trap for the monster.
   - ☐ b. strengthen the hall's doors with iron bands.
   - ☐ c. send for Beowulf.

2. Grendel's face was
   - ☐ a. green and scaly.
   - ☐ b. covered with slime.
   - ☐ c. purple and swollen.

3. Throughout the fight, Beowulf never let go of
   Grendel's
   - ☐ a. throat.
   - ☐ b. wrist.
   - ☐ c. hair.

4. Grendel was badly hurt by
   - ☐ a. burning coals from the fireplace.
   - ☐ b. the thrusting of the warriors' swords and
     spears.
   - ☐ c. Beowulf's dagger.

5. Beowulf wrenched out the monster's arm when he
   and Grendel
   - ☐ a. fell into the fireplace.
   - ☐ b. got to the swamp.
   - ☐ c. reached the doorway.

Score 5 points for each correct answer

____ TOTAL SCORE: Recalling Facts

C MAKING INFERENCES

An inference is a judgment that is made or an idea that is
arrived at based on facts or on information that is given. You
make an inference when you understand something that is *not*
stated directly, but that is *implied*, or suggested by the facts that
are given.

Below are five statements that are judgments or ideas that
have been arrived at from the facts of the story. Write the letter
C in the box in front of each statement that is a correct inference. Write the letter *F* in front of each faulty inference.

C—Correct Inference   F—Faulty Inference

____ ☐ 1. The chief activity of Vikings was the robbing and
         plundering of cities and ships.

____ ☐ 2. Grendel was about twenty feet tall.

____ ☐ 3. Grendel's chief food was the slime and other
         plants of the swamp.

____ ☐ 4. Beowulf usually fought without wearing armor.

____ ☐ 5. Beowulf believed in fighting fairly.

Score 5 points for each correct answer

____ TOTAL SCORE: Making Inferences

D USING WORDS PRECISELY

Each of the numbered sentences below contains an underlined word or phrase from the story you have just read. Under the sentence are three definitions. One has the *same* meaning as the underlined word or phrase, one has *almost the same* meaning, and one has the *opposite* meaning. Match the definitions with the three answer choices by writing the letter that stands for each answer in the box in front of the definition it goes with.

S—Same   A—Almost the Same   O—Opposite

1. It was a swollen purple mass with eyes that regarded the world with pure hatred.

   ___ ☐ a. examined

   ___ ☐ b. looked upon

   ___ ☐ c. turned away from

2. As the men fought in vain, Grendel's iron claws slashed through their shields and armor.

   ___ ☐ a. successfully

   ___ ☐ b. uselessly

   ___ ☐ c. dejectedly

3. He said to his men, "I will strive against this fiend weaponless."

   ___ ☐ a. struggle

   ___ ☐ b. work

   ___ ☐ c. give in

4. They remained clothed in their heavy armor, in anticipation of a great struggle.

   ___ ☐ a. expectation

   ___ ☐ b. hope

   ___ ☐ c. uncertainty

5. Back in the hall, Beowulf stood exhausted, still holding the monster's severed arm.

   ___ ☐ a. injured

   ___ ☐ b. attached

   ___ ☐ c. torn off

___ Score 3 points for each correct *S* answer

___ Score 1 point for each correct *A* or *O* answer

___ TOTAL SCORE: Using Words Precisely

● *Enter the four total scores in the spaces below, and add them together to find your Critical Reading Score. Then record your Critical Reading Score on the graph on page 157.*

_____ Finding the Main Idea
_____ Recalling Facts
_____ Making Inferences
_____ Using Words Precisely

_____ CRITICAL READING SCORE: Unit 15

The sea is calm, and a fresh breeze moves the sailing vessel along. Suddenly the ship begins to rock and the water to foam. From beneath the waves, great tentacles thrust their way to the sky, then move to encircle the ship and drag terrified sailors to their deaths. Such were the tales of the sailors of long ago. But there aren't really sea monsters, are there? Well, there is still a great deal that is not known about life in the deepest parts of the oceans. But scientists do know that there is a sea creature that comes pretty close to meeting the descriptions given by the sailing men of long ago. It is called the kraken.

The Kraken

For hundreds of years, sailors have told of the strange and wondrous creatures that live in the sea. Stories have been told of sea monsters that swallowed up whole fleets. There have been tales of underwater beasts with arms so long they could encircle even the biggest ship. Ancient maps of the sea actually provided illustrations of the monsters. Drawings on the maps showed unexplored waters filled with huge and terrifying sea monsters.

Today the sea still contains many mysteries. Creatures as yet unknown to us may well be living in the depths of the oceans. While many mysteries remain, however, we do know much more about the creatures of the sea than the early explorers did.

We are quite sure that what sailors called monsters were really huge octopuses and giant squid. The giant octopus has a large head and eight long tentacles attached to its body. Each tentacle has two rows of powerful suckers. The giant squid has a long, tapered body and ten arms. As with the octopus, each arm has suckers. The suckers are ringed with teeth. They can be dangerous weapons. Both the octopus and the squid are such large, slimy, repulsive creatures that it is little wonder they were labeled monsters.

Norwegian fishermen had a different name for the hideous creatures. They called them *kraken*. Today that name is applied to all giant squid. In the late 1700s, the Bishop of Bergen, Norway, described the kraken this way: "The kraken is . . . incontestably the largest sea monster in the world." The bishop went on to say that the back of the kraken "seems to be a mile and a half in circumference . . . [and] looks at first like a number of small islands . . . . Several bright points appear. [These] grow thicker and thicker the higher they rise above the surface of the water, and sometimes they stand up as high and as large as the masts of middle-sized vessels."

Despite the bishop's colorful language, modern readers can recognize this kraken as a giant squid or octopus. In fact, we can see the giant squid and its octopus cousin in many old accounts of sea monsters. We can even discern squid and octopuses in Homer's three-thousand-year-old tale of Ulysses and the sea monster called Scylla.

According to Homer's story, Ulysses and his men were returning to Greece by ship when they reached an especially dangerous stretch of water. To continue, they had to sail through a narrow passage between two perils. One was Charybdis, a rapidly-spinning whirlpool whose suction no ship could possibly escape. The other was Scylla, a monster that lived in a cave in the nearby rocks. Ships trying to avoid the waters of the whirlpool always fell victim to Scylla.

Scylla was a hideous creature with twelve legs and six heads. Each of her terrible heads had three rows of teeth. From her mouth came a sharp barking noise that never ceased. The rest of her body was made up of doglike monsters. Scylla was an absolute terror to ships and sailors. Her body remained hidden in her cave, but whenever a ship passed, each of her heads would seize one crew member. Although Ulysses was a brave warrior and a clever fellow, neither his courage nor his cunning could prevent Scylla from demolishing his crew.

As Ulysses sailed his ship through the narrow passage, he passed close to Scylla's cave to avoid the whirlpool. He knew that no ship caught up in that maelstrom had ever gotten out in one piece. Ulysses' crew watched the frightful cone of spinning waters, anticipating disaster at any moment. Disaster did strike, but it did not come from the whirling waters.

Ulysses tells the story of what happened: "Scylla snatched out of my boat the six ablest hands I had on board. I swung 'round, to glance at the ship and run my eye over the crew, just in time to see the arms and legs of her victims dangled high in the air above my head. 'Ulysses!' they called out to me in their agony. But it was the last time they used my name. For like an angler . . . gets a bite and whips his struggling prize to land, Scylla had whisked my comrades up and swept them struggling to the rocks. [There] she devoured them at her own door, [with them] shrieking and stretching out their hands to me in their last desperate throes. In all I have gone through as I made my way across the seas, I have never had to witness a more pitiable sight than that."

As exaggerated as Homer's tale is, his stories were based on real facts and events in Greek history. When we examine this tale for its grain of truth, we can see that the many-headed Scylla was probably a giant squid or an octopus. Her doglike body and constant barking might well have been a colony of harbor seals gathered near her on the rocks. And the monster's three rows of teeth could have been the menacing teeth of a shark.

Although Homer's account of Scylla might seem fanciful and overly dramatic, modern encounters with giant squid prove that they really are quite fearsome. In 1861, the French warship *Alecton*, traveling near the Canary Islands, ran into a monstrous sea serpent. The ship's captain thought the creature might be a giant squid, and he resolved to capture it. He ordered his sailors to fire rifle shots at it, but the bullets seemed to have no effect on the creature. Eventually the crew managed to harpoon it. After securing a noose around its tail, the sailors tried to swing the beast on board the ship. As they hoisted it up, it waved its many arms frantically. In doing so, the creature managed to break the harpoon and pull most of its body free of the ropes. The crew was left holding only a tiny portion of the creature's tail. When they hauled it aboard, however, they found that even that small piece weighed forty pounds.

Incidents such as that have helped modern scientists gather information about giant squid and octopuses. Studying captive whales has also helped us learn about real "sea monsters." A captive whale living in an aquarium once vomited two octopus tentacles. By examining the tentacles, experts were able to calculate the size and weight of the octopus from which they had come. The octopus must have been at least sixty-six feet long, and it is believed to have weighed an incredible eighty-five thousand pounds.

Some sperm whales that have been captured bear the scars of a squid's attack. The tooth-ringed suckers of a squid leave visible marks on their victims. By studying those marks, scientists have added to our knowledge of squid. We now know that while sperm whales are happy to eat giant squid, the giant squid are equally happy to devour sperm whales.

The underwater battles between those two enemies must be ferocious, for both creatures are enormous. The largest elephants weigh only eight tons. Sperm whales grow to a length of sixty-nine feet and can weigh up to sixty tons. Giant squid are even bigger. A fifty-foot squid will leave a ring of tooth marks that measures three to four inches across. Now think of this: sperm whales have been found with sucker marks that are eighteen inches across! That means that the squid that left them was at least two hundred feet long!

As we continue to unravel the mysteries of the sea, we will probably learn more about the giant squid and huge octopuses that inhabit the depths of the oceans. For now, though, it is enough to remember that those ancient sailors who reported seeing hideous sea monsters hadn't just been out to sea too long. ■

If you have been timed while reading this selection, enter your reading time below. Then turn to the Words per Minute table on page 155 and look up your reading speed (words per minute). Enter your reading speed on the graph on page 156.

READING TIME: Unit 16

_____ : _____

Minutes   *Seconds*

How well did you read?

- *Answer the four types of questions that follow. The directions for each type of question tell you how to mark your answers.*

- *When you have finished all four exercises, check your work by using the answer key on page 152. For each right answer, put a check mark (✔) on the line beside the box. For each wrong answer, write the correct answer on the line.*

- *For scoring each exercise, follow the directions below the questions.*

A FINDING THE MAIN IDEA

Look at the three statements below. One expresses the main idea of the story you just read. A good main idea statement answers two questions: it tells *who* or *what* is the subject of the story, and it answers the understood question *does what?* or *is what?* Another statement is *too broad*, it is vague and doesn't tell much about the topic of the story. The third statement is *too narrow*, it tells about only one part of the story.

Match the statements with the three answer choices below by writing the letter of each answer in the box in front of the statement it goes with.

M—Main Idea   **B—Too Broad**   **N—Too Narrow**

____ ☐ 1. Ancient tales of giant sea monsters with long, powerful arms have a strong basis in the characteristics of giant squid and octopuses.

____ ☐ 2. There is reliable evidence of squid as large as two hundred feet long.

____ ☐ 3. Tales of giant sea monsters, which go back to the Greeks, have a basis in scientific fact.

____ Score 15 points for a correct *M* answer

____ Score 5 points for each correct *B* or *N* answer

____ TOTAL SCORE: Finding the Main Idea

B RECALLING FACTS

How well do you remember the facts in the story you just read? Put an x in the box in front of the correct answer to each of the multiple-choice questions below.

1. Ulysses had to choose between sailing near a sea monster and risking his ship to
   - ☐ a. an octopus.
   - ☐ b. a whirlpool.
   - ☐ c. crashing waves.

2. Kraken are probably actually
   - ☐ a. the descendants of prehistoric sea creatures.
   - ☐ b. huge jellyfish.
   - ☐ c. giant squid and octopuses.

3. The French sailors who tried to catch what they thought was a sea serpent got
   - ☐ a. a piece of its tail.
   - ☐ b. only its head.
   - ☐ c. nothing.

4. The size of some giant squid has been determined by
   - ☐ a. measurements taken from photos that have been snapped of the creatures at sea.
   - ☐ b. the size of the sucker marks they left on whales.
   - ☐ c. historical accounts of encounters with the creatures.

5. Both the giant octopus and the giant squid have
   - ☐ a. large teeth in their mouths.
   - ☐ b. eight tentacles.
   - ☐ c. suckers.

Score 5 points for each correct answer

_____ TOTAL SCORE: Recalling Facts

C MAKING INFERENCES

An inference is a judgment that is made or an idea that is arrived at based on facts or on information that is given. You make an inference when you understand something that is *not* stated directly, but that is *implied,* or suggested by the facts that are given.

Below are five statements that are judgments or ideas that have been arrived at from the facts of the story. Write the letter C in the box in front of each statement that is a correct inference. Write the letter F in front of each faulty inference.

C—Correct Inference   F—Faulty Inference

_____ ☐ 1. The Bishop of Bergen, Norway, saw the largest sea monster ever reported—the Kraken.

_____ ☐ 2. Ulysses would have lost his entire crew if he had tried to avoid Scylla.

_____ ☐ 3. Sperm whales live on a diet of only squid and octopus.

_____ ☐ 4. Sperm whales and squid have few natural enemies.

_____ ☐ 5. Scientists can learn a great deal about an animal by studying just a small part of it.

Score 5 points for each correct answer

_____ TOTAL SCORE: Making Inferences

D USING WORDS PRECISELY

Each of the numbered sentences below contains an underlined word or phrase from the story you have just read. Under the sentence are three definitions. One has the *same* meaning as the underlined word or phrase, one has *almost the same* meaning, and one has the *opposite* meaning. Match the definitions with the three answer choices by writing the letter that stands for each answer in the box in front of the definition it goes with.

S—Same   A—Almost the Same   O—Opposite

1. Both the octopus and the squid are such large, slimy, <u>repulsive</u> creatures that it is little wonder they were labeled monsters.

   ____ ☐ a. disgusting

   ____ ☐ b. appealing

   ____ ☐ c. unattractive

2. To continue, they had to sail through a narrow passage between two <u>perils</u>.

   ____ ☐ a. frightful places

   ____ ☐ b. safe places

   ____ ☐ c. dangers

3. He knew that no ship caught up in that <u>maelstrom</u> had ever gotten out in one piece.

   ____ ☐ a. stormy seas

   ____ ☐ b. whirlpool

   ____ ☐ c. calm waters

4. Although Ulysses was a brave warrior and a clever fellow, neither his courage nor his <u>cunning</u> could prevent Scylla from demolishing his crew.

   ____ ☐ a. brilliance

   ____ ☐ b. cleverness

   ____ ☐ c. lack of imagination

5. The ship's captain thought the creature might be a giant squid, and he <u>resolved</u> to capture it.

   ____ ☐ a. determined

   ____ ☐ b. vowed

   ____ ☐ c. hesitated

____ Score 3 points for each correct S answer
____ Score 1 point for each correct A or O answer

____ TOTAL SCORE: Using Words Precisely

● *Enter the four total scores in the spaces below, and add them together to find your Critical Reading Score. Then record your Critical Reading Score on the graph on page 157.*

_____	Finding the Main Idea
_____	Recalling Facts
_____	Making Inferences
_____	Using Words Precisely
_____	**CRITICAL READING SCORE: Unit 16**

Bela Lugosi, the most chilling film Dracula of all time, prepares to drain the blood from yet another innocent victim. The familiar story of the bloodsucking count was written as a novel by Bram Stoker in 1897. The basis for this vampire story, however, goes back much further, to a real time and place and to a real Count Dracula.

Dracula

They come in the night, flying from their graves in the form of bats. If they are not stopped, they will kill the members of their own families, and then go on to take the lives of others. They are vampires—corpses that rise from their coffins in the middle of the night, seeking out living victims whose blood they drink to sustain their unnatural existence.

The most famous of all vampires is Count Dracula, a fictional character made famous in books and movies. Dracula is portrayed as a tall, dark figure with two long fangs. He wears a black cape lined with red silk. As is true of all vampires, he can abandon his coffin only after the sun has set, and he must return to it before sunrise, for he cannot survive in the light of day. He attacks his victims by piercing their necks with his fangs and sucking out their blood. A vampire's victims also become vampires (although according to some stories, it takes three bites to bring that about).

Like Count Dracula, a newly created vampire will live forever, roaming the lands in the dark of night to find its own victims. There is only one way the monster can be stopped: someone must drive a wooden stake through its heart.

Although the legend of Dracula the vampire is not true, there was once a real Count Dracula. Like the vampire of fiction and film, he lived in the mountainous part of eastern Europe known as Transylvania. He was born to nobility in 1431, and while his real name was Vlad, he was called by his nickname, Dracula, which means "son of the dragon." He was also known as Vlad the Impaler, a nickname he earned for the barbaric acts he committed.

In the fifteenth century, Turkish warriors were conquering much of southeastern Europe. When Dracula was thirteen, the Turks captured his father. In order to secure his own freedom, the father gave Dracula to the Turks as a hostage. For the next four years, Dracula was imprisoned in a Turkish jail.

Perhaps it was his father's betrayal that warped Dracula's mind, but whatever the reason, from 1448 on, Dracula was renowned as a fierce and evil madman. After his imprisonment, he returned to rule his native Transylvania. His main job was to defend it against the Turks, and he himself led many battles against the invaders. But he also murdered thousands of his own countrymen. There was usually no reason for the killings except that they gave Dracula pleasure.

His favorite method of killing was impalement. Many times he ordered his servants to prepare hundreds of long wooden stakes. He wanted the tips of the stakes to be rounded a bit—not so sharp that his victims would die quickly. Then the torture would begin. Dracula would order the stakes to be driven through the entire lengths of his victims' bodies. The stakes would later be erected on the hills around the town, and the maimed people would be left there to suffer a slow and agonizing death.

For several years, Dracula terrorized the people of Transylvania with such monstrous deeds. Perhaps his single greatest crime occurred on the morning of August 24, 1460. On that day, Dracula ordered thirty thousand Transylvanians impaled on stakes around the city of Brasov.

Dracula's crazed acts also had a powerful effect on the invading Turks. As an army of Turks approached one Transylvanian town in 1460, they were horrified by what they saw. There outside the city were the remains of twenty thousand men rotting on wooden stakes. The men, most of whom were members of the upper class, had been Dracula's prisoners. All had offended Dracula in some way. Repulsed by the sight, the Turks turned away.

At last the Turks did succeed in invading Transylvania and capturing Dracula.

Although his rule was ended, word of his gruesome deeds lived on and soon became legend.

One other historical figure whose habits became part of the vampire legend was Countess Elizabeth Bathory. Also from Transylvania, she lived during the seventeenth century. One day a maid who was combing Elizabeth's hair pulled one strand a little too hard. Angered, the countess slapped the girl so forcefully that blood appeared on the girl's cheek. A few drops of the blood splattered onto the countess's hand, and to Elizabeth's twisted mind, the blood seemed to have the effect of making her skin as firm and fresh as that of the young maid. The countess quickly summoned her servants and ordered the girl killed so that her blood could be drained into a tub. Elizabeth bathed in the blood and believed that it made her look younger.

Over the next ten years, the countess had many young maidens killed in order to bathe in their blood. Finally one day a girl escaped and ran to notify the king. It was only then that the countess was arrested and her grisly ritual halted.

Stories about such characters as Elizabeth Bathory and Vlad the Impaler were passed down through the years, eventually becoming part of the general folklore of eastern Europe. The legend of Dracula was brought to the West by Bram Stoker, who in the late 1800s wrote the first novel about the vampire.

Since then, interest in Dracula has grown in both western Europe and America. Over a hundred vampire films have been made. Bela Lugosi was the first American movie Dracula, and he remains the most famous. Lugosi so loved the role that in his will he requested that he be buried in his Dracula costume, cape and all. ∎

If you have been timed while reading this selection, enter your reading time below. Then turn to the Words per Minute table on page 155 and look up your reading speed (words per minute). Enter your reading speed on the graph on page 156.

READING TIME: Unit 17

_____ : _____
Minutes   *Seconds*

How well did you read?

- *Answer the four types of questions that follow. The directions for each type of question tell you how to mark your answers.*

- *When you have finished all four exercises, check your work by using the answer key on page 152. For each right answer, put a check mark (✔) on the line beside the box. For each wrong answer, write the correct answer on the line.*

- *For scoring each exercise, follow the directions below the questions.*

A FINDING THE MAIN IDEA

Look at the three statements below. One expresses the main idea of the story you just read. A good main idea statement answers two questions: it tells *who* or *what* is the subject of the story, and it answers the understood question *does what?* or *is what?* Another statement is *too broad,* it is vague and doesn't tell much about the topic of the story. The third statement is *too narrow,* it tells about only one part of the story.

Match the statements with the three answer choices below by writing the letter of each answer in the box in front of the statement it goes with.

M—Main Idea   **B—Too Broad**   **N—Too Narrow**

_____ ☐ 1. The fictional vampire Count Dracula was a mix of the insane traits of some real people.

_____ ☐ 2. The fictional vampire Count Dracula is based on a real Transylvanian Dracula and a mad Transylvanian countess.

_____ ☐ 3. In Transylvania in the fifteenth century, there was a real Count Dracula, whose nickname was Vlad the Impaler.

_____ Score 15 points for a correct *M* answer

_____ Score 5 points for each correct *B* or *N* answer

_____ TOTAL SCORE: Finding the Main Idea

B RECALLING FACTS

How well do you remember the facts in the story you just read? Put an x in the box in front of the correct answer to each of the multiple-choice questions below.

1. Vlad the Impaler was
   - ___ ☐ a. the ruler of Transylvania.
   - ___ ☐ b. a barbaric Turk.
   - ___ ☐ c. the father of Countess Elizabeth Bathory.

2. Vlad got rid of Turkish invaders by
   - ___ ☐ a. offering them hostages.
   - ___ ☐ b. impaling them.
   - ___ ☐ c. erecting impaled victims for them to see.

3. The most famous Dracula of the movies was
   - ___ ☐ a. Lon Chaney.
   - ___ ☐ b. Bela Lugosi.
   - ___ ☐ c. Vincent Price.

4. Countess Elizabeth Bathory
   - ___ ☐ a. bathed in blood.
   - ___ ☐ b. drank blood.
   - ___ ☐ c. pierced the necks of her young maids.

5. Countess Elizabeth Bathory lived in
   - ___ ☐ a. England.
   - ___ ☐ b. Transylvania.
   - ___ ☐ c. France.

Score 5 points for each correct answer

___ TOTAL SCORE: Recalling Facts

C MAKING INFERENCES

An inference is a judgment that is made or an idea that is arrived at based on facts or on information that is given. You make an inference when you understand something that is *not* stated directly, but that is *implied*, or suggested by the facts that are given.

Below are five statements that are judgments or ideas that have been arrived at from the facts of the story. Write the letter C in the box in front of each statement that is a correct inference. Write the letter F in front of each faulty inference.

C—Correct Inference   F—Faulty Inference

- ___ ☐ 1. The Turks who finally conquered Transylvania were kind rulers.

- ___ ☐ 2. The people of Transylvania felt that they were powerless to stop Count Dracula.

- ___ ☐ 3. Vlad became insane because of the torture he underwent during his four years in a Turkish jail.

- ___ ☐ 4. Some of Countess Elizabeth Bathory's servants helped her continue her ghastly ritual of bathing in blood.

- ☐ 5. Bram Stoker, who wrote the first novel about Count Dracula, believed in the existence of vampires.

Score 5 points for each correct answer

___ TOTAL SCORE: Making Inferences

D USING WORDS PRECISELY

Each of the numbered sentences below contains an underlined word or phrase from the story you have just read. Under the sentence are three definitions. One has the *same* meaning as the underlined word or phrase, one has *almost the same* meaning, and one has the *opposite* meaning. Match the definitions with the three answer choices by writing the letter that stands for each answer in the box in front of the definition it goes with.

S—Same   A—Almost the Same   O—Opposite

1. They are vampires—corpses that rise from their coffins in the middle of the night, seeking out living victims whose blood they drink to <u>sustain</u> their unnatural existence.

   ____ ☐ a. allow

   ____ ☐ b. continue

   ____ ☐ c. end

2. In order to <u>secure</u> his own freedom, the father gave Dracula to the Turks as a hostage.

   ____ ☐ a. gain

   ____ ☐ b. keep

   ____ ☐ c. lose

3. <u>Repulsed</u> by the sight, the Turks turned away.

   ____ ☐ a. upset

   ____ ☐ b. disgusted

   ____ ☐ c. attracted

4. Perhaps it was his father's betrayal that warped Dracula's mind, but whatever the reason, from 1448 on, Dracula was <u>renowned</u> as a fierce and evil madman.

   ____ ☐ a. secretly said to be

   ____ ☐ b. applauded

   ____ ☐ c. widely known

5. It was only then that the countess was arrested and her <u>grisly</u> ritual halted.

   ____ ☐ a. ghastly

   ____ ☐ b. distasteful

   ____ ☐ c. appealing

____ Score 3 points for each correct S answer
____ Score 1 point for each correct A or O answer

____ TOTAL SCORE: Using Words Precisely

● *Enter the four total scores in the spaces below, and add them together to find your Critical Reading Score. Then record your Critical Reading Score on the graph on page 157.*

_____ Finding the Main Idea
_____ Recalling Facts
_____ Making Inferences
_____ Using Words Precisely
_____ CRITICAL READING SCORE: Unit 17

Clairvius Narcisse is sitting on his own grave, in which he was buried in 1962. How is such a thing possible? Narcisse was a zombie—one of the walking dead. While some people living in Haiti believe that zombies are created through voodoo magic, Narcisse testified that there are other, much less mysterious powers at work.

The Walking Dead

In Haiti some years ago, a group of girls on a shopping trip stepped into a store. As they looked around, a salesgirl walked over to wait on them. When the girls saw the salesgirl, they recognized her as an old friend. But instead of being happy to meet someone they knew, the girls were terrified. The salesgirl had been dead for three years!

Most people in that situation might have assumed that the salesgirl simply bore a close resemblance to their dead friend. But the girls were Haitian and, like a good number of people in Haiti, they believed in another explanation. They believed that the salesgirl was a zombie.

A zombie is someone who is supposedly not alive but not exactly dead either. Zombies are believed to be people who have died and been buried, but who have later been raised from their graves and turned into slaves. For that reason, they are sometimes referred to as the "walking dead." Their gaze is usually a blank stare, and their movements are slow and mechanical. They can work, but only at simple jobs that don't call for any thought. They do only what they are told to do.

Belief in zombies is tied to a belief in voodoo, a religion that developed in Africa. When Africans were brought to the New World as slaves, they brought voodoo with them. Many of those African slaves were taken to the Caribbean island of Haiti, and even today, long after the end of slavery in Haiti, voodoo is practiced on the island. Although voodoo has spread to parts of both North and South America, Haiti remains the center for voodoo.

The most powerful person in the world of voodoo is the houngan, or voodoo priest. Houngans are said to have many powers. Among them is the power to raise the dead. It is the houngan who commands corpses to rise from their graves, and it is he who turns the corpses into zombies. Once a zombie has been created, the houngan has absolute control over him or her. Zombies have no minds of their own; they will do only what the houngan commands them. If he tells them to walk, they will walk. If he orders them to pick sugar cane, that is what they will do. Frequently a houngan uses his zombies to do farm work for him, and occasionally he rents them out to other farmers.

Most of the stories about zombies come from poor, uneducated people. Skeptics point out that in Haiti people in those circumstances tend to be very superstitious, and therefore, they are not the most reliable sources. But a well-educated man told the following story of meeting a zombie. The man was driving in the country when his car broke down in front of a house he had never noticed before. The owner of the house, a houngan, invited the man inside. The houngan explained that he had caused the car to break down because he wanted the man to meet somebody. The houngan then brought out a zombie. The startled man recognized the zombie as a friend he hadn't seen in a year.

Another Haitian zombie was seen by many people and was even photographed. Her story is famous. She showed up one day on a farm where people recognized her. The people remembered her as a relative of the owner of the farm. They also remembered that she had died several years earlier. Everyone who had known the woman was sure that it was the same person. The people accused the dead woman's husband of poisoning his wife and then paying a houngan to turn her into a zombie. The mystery has never been cleared up, and some people continue to believe that voodoo is responsible for this bizarre occurrence. Others, however, have suggested other explanations.

One possibility is that the dead woman's relatives had hired an impostor to pose as the zombie. If they hated the dead woman's husband and wanted to get him in trouble, that was one way to do it. Accusing him of conspiring with a houngan was a sure way of making trouble for him.

Another explanation is that the woman had never died, but had been drugged by the houngan. In a heavily drugged state, she had been believed dead. A few hours after she was buried, the houngan dug her up again and made her his slave. He kept her drugged from then on, in order to keep her in his power. Many people who have studied voodoo believe that this is how zombies are made. The houngans have great power in the eyes of those who believe in voodoo. His followers do not question his ability to raise the dead. They both fear and respect him.

Some zombies have been proved to be fakes. One investigator, for instance, tells of accompanying a houngan and his assistant to a graveyard to watch them create a zombie. First the assistant dug up a coffin and opened it. The houngan uttered some magic words over the body and poured a liquid on it. Then the corpse sat up, got out of the coffin and, moving as though in a trance, walked away with the houngan. The whole thing looked real, but the investigator was suspicious.

The next day, the investigator went back to the cemetery for another look at the empty grave. As he looked around, he discovered an air hose leading down to where the coffin had been. When he saw that, he realized that the creation of the zombie had been a trick. The "zombie" had never been dead. Rather, a living person had been lying in the coffin, breathing through the air hose and waiting to be dug up.

Most Haitians don't believe in zombies, but those who do have influenced the country's burial customs. It is said that the families of some dead people take turns guarding the graves of their loved ones. They stand guard for several weeks after the person has been buried. Only then do they feel it is safe to end their vigil. They figure that by then the corpse is too decomposed to be of use to any houngan who might want to turn it into a slave.

Is there really such a thing as voodoo magic? Voodoo exists as long as people believe in it. By believing in the houngans, the people give them power, just as a magician works real magic in the eyes of trusting and innocent children. ■

If you have been timed while reading this selection, enter your reading time below. Then turn to the Words per Minute table on page 155 and look up your reading speed (words per minute). Enter your reading speed on the graph on page 156.

READING TIME: Unit 18

_____ : _____

Minutes   *Seconds*

How well did you read?

- *Answer the four types of questions that follow. The directions for each type of question tell you how to mark your answers.*

- *When you have finished all four exercises, check your work by using the answer key on page 152. For each right answer, put a check mark (✔) on the line beside the box. For each wrong answer, write the correct answer on the line.*

- *For scoring each exercise, follow the directions below the questions.*

A FINDING THE MAIN IDEA

Look at the three statements below. One expresses the main idea of the story you just read. A good main idea statement answers two questions: it tells *who* or *what* is the subject of the story, and it answers the understood question *does what?* or *is what?* Another statement is *too broad,* it is vague and doesn't tell much about the topic of the story. The third statement is *too narrow,* it tells about only one part of the story.

Match the statements with the three answer choices below by writing the letter of each answer in the box in front of the statement it goes with.

M—Main Idea   B—Too Broad   N—Too Narrow

____ ☐ 1. People who believe in voodoo believe that voodoo priests can create zombies—raise dead people and have power over them.

____ ☐ 2. Some people believe that zombies are actually people who have been heavily drugged by voodoo priests.

____ ☐ 3. Zombies, or the "walking dead," are part of the religion called voodoo.

____ Score 15 points for a correct *M* answer
____ Score 5 points for each correct *B* or *N* answer
____ TOTAL SCORE: Finding the Main Idea

B RECALLING FACTS

How well do you remember the facts in the story you just read? Put an *x* in the box in front of the correct answer to each of the multiple-choice questions below.

1. Houngans frequently use zombies
   - ☐ a. to serve as their assistants.
   - ☐ b. as robots.
   - ☐ c. to work their farms.

2. The investigator who saw a houngan dig up a coffin and raise the corpse discovered that
   - ☐ a. the "corpse" had never been dead.
   - ☐ b. the houngan had drugged the dead man.
   - ☐ c. the "corpse" was a hired actor.

3. To keep their dead relatives from being turned into zombies, some Haitians
   - ☐ a. guard the graves until the corpses have decayed.
   - ☐ b. delay burying their dead for several weeks.
   - ☐ c. refuse to bury their dead.

4. Voodoo originated in
   - ☐ a. South America.
   - ☐ b. Haiti.
   - ☐ c. Africa.

5. Most investigators who have studied voodoo believe that houngans
   - ☐ a. can truly raise the dead.
   - ☐ b. drug all their believers.
   - ☐ c. fool people.

Score 5 points for each correct answer

____ TOTAL SCORE: Recalling Facts

C MAKING INFERENCES

An inference is a judgment that is made or an idea that is arrived at based on facts or on information that is given. You make an inference when you understand something that is *not* stated directly, but that is *implied*, or suggested by the facts that are given.

Below are five statements that are judgments or ideas that have been arrived at from the facts of the story. Write the letter *C* in the box in front of each statement that is a correct inference. Write the letter *F* in front of each faulty inference.

C—Correct Inference   F—Faulty Inference

____ ☐ 1. People who guard the graves of their dead have complete faith in the powers of the houngans.

____ ☐ 2. Houngans believe that they have supernatural powers.

____ ☐ 3. The element of fear plays a large part in the voodoo religion.

____ ☐ 4. Belief in voodoo is beginning to spread.

____ ☐ 5. People who have been heavily drugged by houngans cannot communicate with other people.

Score 5 points for each correct answer

____ TOTAL SCORE: Making Inferences

D USING WORDS PRECISELY

Each of the numbered sentences below contains an underlined word or phrase from the story you have just read. Under the sentence are three definitions. One has the *same* meaning as the underlined word or phrase, one has *almost the same* meaning, and one has the *opposite* meaning. Match the definitions with the three answer choices by writing the letter that stands for each answer in the box in front of the definition it goes with.

S—Same   A—Almost the Same   O—Opposite

1. Their gaze is usually a blank stare, and their movements are slow and mechanical.

____ ☐ a. uninterested

____ ☐ b. without expression

____ ☐ c. lively

2. The mystery has never been cleared up, and some people continue to believe that voodoo is responsible for this bizarre occurrence.

____ ☐ a. odd

____ ☐ b. unusual

____ ☐ c. ordinary

3. Accusing him of conspiring with a houngan was a sure way of making trouble for him.

____ ☐ a. acting openly

____ ☐ b. associating

____ ☐ c. plotting

4. Only then do they feel it is safe to end their vigil.

____ ☐ a. constant watch

____ ☐ b. frequent observation

____ ☐ c. avoidance

5. They figure that by then the corpse is too decomposed to be of use to any houngan who might want to turn it into a slave.

____ ☐ a. whole

____ ☐ b. dilapidated

____ ☐ c. decayed

____ Score 3 points for each correct S answer
____ Score 1 point for each correct A or O answer

____ TOTAL SCORE: Using Words Precisely

● *Enter the four total scores in the spaces below, and add them together to find your Critical Reading Score. Then record your Critical Reading Score on the graph on page 157.*

_____ Finding the Main Idea
_____ Recalling Facts
_____ Making Inferences
_____ Using Words Precisely

_____ CRITICAL READING SCORE: Unit 18

Werewolves

In the mid 1700s, a brutal murder shook the quiet mountainous region of south-central France. There, in an isolated mountain pasture in the area known as Le Gevaudan, a young shepherd girl was found dead. That news alone was enough to shock the simple peasant families of the area. But when the cause of death was revealed, a panic spread throughout the region. The girl's heart had been torn out of her chest.

It turned out that that horrible murder was only the beginning. Within days, another child was killed, and then another and another. At that time, many of the children of Le Gevaudan were working as shepherds. So it was the children, alone in the mountains, who fell victim to the mad killer that became known as the Beast of Le Gevaudan.

Finally, after several children had been murdered, things seemed to return to normal. Weeks passed with no additional murders. The peace of the area was again shattered, however, when a peasant woman from a nearby village began spreading a frightening tale. The woman said that she had been caring for her cattle with the help of her guard dogs, when suddenly a terrible creature appeared and began to threaten the cattle. According to the woman, the creature was as big as a donkey but walked on two legs, like a person. It was covered with short reddish hair and had a snout like a pig. It was so ferocious that the woman's dogs were terrified of it. Instead of chasing the creature away, as they were trained to do, the dogs turned and ran, leaving the woman and her cattle at the mercy of the beast. Luckily, when the monster approached the cattle, the cows lowered their horns and attacked, causing the beast to flee.

When the people of Le Gevaudan heard the woman's story, they weren't sure what to think. To most of them, the idea of an animal that could scare off guard dogs sounded preposterous. But their disbelief soon vanished. A local hunter known for his dependability and truthfulness reported seeing the same animal that the woman had described. The hunter explained that he had tried to shoot the creature but that his shot had done no good. He wasn't sure if he had missed or if his bullet had simply had no effect on the beast.

Right after the hunter reported the incident, the killings began again. More young children were found dead in the fields, their hearts torn from their bodies. The terrified people of Le Gevaudan concluded that the killer must be the monstrous creature that had been seen by the hunter and the peasant woman from the neighboring town. In desperation, the villagers announced that children would no longer be allowed to herd sheep up to the mountain pastures. Everyone also stopped going out after dark. And whenever the people of the town did gather together, they talked of nothing but the loup-garou, "the werewolf," that was killing their children.

It did not take long for stories of the loup-garou to reach the French king. He sent a detachment of soldiers to search for and destroy the beast. Almost as soon as the soldiers entered Le Gevaudan, they encountered the creature. Quickly they fired on it, but it disappeared into the woods without leaving a trace. The soldiers searched the local forests carefully, but found neither the living creature nor its body. At last the troops were convinced that they had mortally wounded the beast and that it had crawled off to some hidden place to die. The soldiers left the area, and their commander reported the success of the mission to the king.

The people of Le Gevaudan were delighted. They began once again to venture out after dark. The children resumed their jobs as shepherds. Everyone in the region breathed a great sigh of relief. Then, without warning, the nightmare began again. Yet another child was found dead.

At about the same time, an enormous wolf was spotted on a mountain in a nearby area. Again the king dispatched a band of soldiers to search for the creature. The troops did find and kill a large wolf that they claimed was the "Beast of Le Gevaudan." The king proudly announced that the loup-garou was dead. But apparently the wolf killed by the soldiers was not the loup-garou, for the killings continued. For the next three years, the monster terrorized the villagers in the area of Le Gevaudan. It left a long trail of mutilated corpses and caused many townspeople to abandon their homes and villages.

Finally a local nobleman decided to organize a monster hunt. The hunters, who vowed not to rest until the beast was dead, succeeded in surrounding the notorious creature in a patch of woods. One hunter fired two silver bullets at the beast, and at long last it fell dead.

The monster was described as a huge wolf with close-cropped ears and hooves for feet. Its carcass was carried from village to village so the people could see that the Beast of Le Gevaudan really was dead. It was early summer, however, and

the heat soon caused the carcass to decay. It was, therefore, necessary to bury it in a hurry. Unfortunately, the quick burial prevented people from making a full study of the creature, so today we do not have many details to help us understand what the beast looked like.

We do know that the people of Le Gevaudan were not the first ones to be frightened by a "werewolf." Even though it was more than two hundred years ago that the Beast of Le Gevaudan terrorized the region, the idea of werewolves was an old one even then.

A folktale from ancient Rome tells of a young man named Niceros who had an encounter with a werewolf. One day Niceros decided to walk to another town to visit a friend. He set off with a young soldier who had offered to go along to keep him company. Soon Niceros realized that his companion was no longer walking by his side. He looked back just in time to see the soldier standing at the edge of the road, his clothes lying in a heap around his feet. As Niceros watched in horror, the soldier turned into a huge wolf and ran off into the woods.

Niceros was badly shaken by what he had seen, and he hurried along to his friend's house. When he arrived there, he learned that a large wolf had just killed several of his friend's sheep. The wolf had gotten away, but not before Niceros's friend had stabbed it in the neck with a spear.

Later, as Niceros was walking home, he passed the place where he had last seen the soldier. The clothes were gone, but the site was marked by a large pool of blood. As soon as Niceros reached his own village, he went to the home of the soldier. He found the soldier lying in bed, with a doctor bandaging a wound on his neck.

The story of Niceros was well-known in the Middle Ages, the period of time between 500 and 1400 A.D. During that period, many suspected werewolves were brought to trial and condemned to death. Some poor souls were executed as werewolves simply because they bore such "signs" as having hair on unusual parts of their bodies. Others were proclaimed werewolves on the basis of eyebrows that grew together in the center of their foreheads or of index fingers that were longer than their middle fingers.

In those dark days, it was believed that people who were in league with the devil could transform themselves into werewolves. The werewolves of the Middle Ages were pictured as regular, four-legged wolves. They were not the sort of half-man, half-wolf creature that we are familiar with from the movies. Hollywood's werewolves have given the old stories some new twists. The idea that a full moon can cause a person to turn into a werewolf is strictly from the movies. So too is the notion that a person bitten by a werewolf will turn into one himself.

All ideas of werewolves, it seems, grew from people's imaginations and from ancient superstitions. The earliest hunting societies often worshiped certain wild animals, which they called their totems. One group might have worshiped a bear, for instance, another a wolf. They believed that they had a special connection with the animal, perhaps even that they were descended from it. They believed that the skins of their totems had magical powers. The men would often put on the skins and perform special ceremonies involving drugs, chants and dances. They thought that the animal's strength, power or courage would be transmitted to them. Some of those men probably even became convinced, through the effects of a combination of drugs and their strong beliefs and desires, that they had become the animal. They would then act like the animal.

Given people's powers of imagination, it's not hard to see how the idea of werewolves developed from such a beginning. ■

If you have been timed while reading this selection, enter your reading time below. Then turn to the Words per Minute table on page 155 and look up your reading speed (words per minute). Enter your reading speed on the graph on page 156.

READING TIME: Unit 19

_____ : _____
Minutes   *Seconds*

How well did you read?

- *Answer the four types of questions that follow. The directions for each type of question tell you how to mark your answers.*

- *When you have finished all four exercises, check your work by using the answer key on page 152. For each right answer, put a check mark (✔) on the line beside the box. For each wrong answer, write the correct answer on the line.*

- *For scoring each exercise, follow the directions below the questions.*

A FINDING THE MAIN IDEA

Look at the three statements below. One expresses the main idea of the story you just read. A good main idea statement answers two questions: it tells *who* or *what* is the subject of the story, and it answers the understood question *does what?* or *is what?* Another statement is *too broad*, it is vague and doesn't tell much about the topic of the story. The third statement is *too narrow*, it tells about only one part of the story.

Match the statements with the three answer choices below by writing the letter of each answer in the box in front of the statement it goes with.

M—Main Idea   B—Too Broad   N—Too Narrow

_____ ☐ 1. In the 1700s, a wild beast that the natives called the loup-garou, or werewolf, terrorized villages in the area of Le Gevaudan, France.

_____ ☐ 2. The idea of werewolves—men that turn into wolves and kill people—has been around for thousands of years.

_____ ☐ 3. People that turn into vicious wild beasts have existed in the folklore of many people for centuries.

_____ Score 15 points for a correct *M* answer

_____ Score 5 points for each correct *B* or *N* answer

_____ TOTAL SCORE: Finding the Main Idea

B RECALLING FACTS

How well do you remember the facts in the story you just read?
Put an x in the box in front of the correct answer to each of the
multiple-choice questions below.

1. The Beast of Le Gevaudan killed mainly
   - ____ ☐ a. sheep.
   - ____ ☐ b. children.
   - ____ ☐ c. soldiers.

2. The soldiers who hunted the loup-garou were sent by
   - ____ ☐ a. the general of the local army.
   - ____ ☐ b. neighbors from a nearby village.
   - ____ ☐ c. the king of France.

3. When he was in the form of a wolf, the Roman
   soldier
   - ____ ☐ a. killed sheep.
   - ____ ☐ b. killed a number of people.
   - ____ ☐ c. attacked a man named Niceros.

4. In the Middle Ages, suspected werewolves were
   - ____ ☐ a. tried in court.
   - ____ ☐ b. executed without trials.
   - ____ ☐ c. put in cages.

5. In the myths and legends of werewolves, the beasts do
   not
   - ____ ☐ a. kill people or animals.
   - ____ ☐ b. enter into agreements with the devil.
   - ____ ☐ c. turn into wolves at the time of the full moon.

Score 5 points for each correct answer

____ TOTAL SCORE: Recalling Facts

C MAKING INFERENCES

An inference is a judgment that is made or an idea that is
arrived at based on facts or on information that is given. You
make an inference when you understand something that is *not*
stated directly, but that is *implied*, or suggested by the facts that
are given.

Below are five statements that are judgments or ideas that
have been arrived at from the facts of the story. Write the letter
C in the box in front of each statement that is a correct inference. Write the letter *F* in front of each faulty inference.

C—Correct Inference   **F—Faulty Inference**

- ____ ☐ 1. The king did not really believe that there was a
  loup-garou, but was just trying to calm the
  people.

- ____ ☐ 2. Werewolves did exist in Europe in the Middle
  Ages.

- ____ ☐ 3. The people of the Middle Ages were suspicious
  and fearful of anyone who looked somewhat
  unusual.

- ____ ☐ 4. Werewolf movies convinced many trusting people
  that werewolves were real creatures.

- ____ ☐ 5. The people of Le Gevaudan stopped herding
  sheep during the years in which the loup-garou
  was on the loose.

Score 5 points for each correct answer

____ TOTAL SCORE: Making Inferences

D USING WORDS PRECISELY

Each of the numbered sentences below contains an underlined word or phrase from the story you have just read. Under the sentence are three definitions. One has the *same* meaning as the underlined word or phrase, one has *almost the same* meaning, and one has the *opposite* meaning. Match the definitions with the three answer choices by writing the letter that stands for each answer in the box in front of the definition it goes with.

S—Same   A—Almost the Same   O—Opposite

1. To most of them, the idea of an animal that could scare off guard dogs sounded <u>preposterous</u>.

___ ☐ a. sensible

___ ☐ b. silly

___ ☐ c. absurd

2. At last the troops were convinced that they had <u>mortally</u> wounded the beast and that it had crawled off to some hidden place to die.

___ ☐ a. fatally

___ ☐ b. not seriously

___ ☐ c. badly

3. The idea that a full moon can cause a person to turn into a werewolf is <u>strictly</u> from the movies.

___ ☐ a. mainly

___ ☐ b. solely

___ ☐ c. partly

4. In those dark days, it was believed that people who were <u>in league with</u> the devil could turn themselves into werewolves.

___ ☐ a. separated from

___ ☐ b. familiar with

___ ☐ c. united with

5. Others were <u>proclaimed</u> werewolves on the basis of eyebrows that grew together or of index fingers that were longer than their middle fingers.

___ ☐ a. not pronounced

___ ☐ b. declared

___ ☐ c. accused

___ Score 3 points for each correct *S* answer

___ Score 1 point for each correct *A* or *O* answer

___ TOTAL SCORE: Using Words Precisely

● *Enter the four total scores in the spaces below, and add them together to find your Critical Reading Score. Then record your Critical Reading Score on the graph on page 157.*

_____ Finding the Main Idea
_____ Recalling Facts
_____ Making Inferences
_____ Using Words Precisely

_____ CRITICAL READING SCORE: Unit 19

They have been glimpsed here and there among the icy peaks of the Himalayas— hairy two-legged creatures traversing the shimmering landscape. Small men in fur coats? Apes of some kind? Natives of the area claim that they are Yetis—wild men of the mountains. But no one has ever gotten close enough to find out for sure just what those elusive shaggy creatures are.

The Yeti

The creature seemed to materialize from nowhere. Suddenly there it was, walking along the frozen ice field high in the Himalayan Mountains. It walked upright on two feet, the shape of its body similar to that of a small man. As it moved, the bright winter sun shimmered on its shaggy fur. Occasionally it stopped and bent to rummage among patches of mountain shrubbery. Then, as quickly as it had come, the creature vanished.

Only a few people witnessed the appearance of the odd creature on that sunny day in 1925. Most were Sherpa guides. Sherpas are natives of Bhutan, Nepal and Tibet, the countries of the Himalayas. Because of their extensive knowledge of the mountains, they often act as guides for the Europeans and Americans who wish to climb in the region. It was on one such climbing expedition that this sighting of the creature took place.

Just what was the mysterious creature? The Sherpas were convinced that it was a Yeti, a wild man of the mountains. For generations, the Sherpas have believed in the existence of small wild men who inhabit the northern pockets of the Himalayas. They believe that Yetis are wanderers—creatures that roam from place to place, with no permanent homes. Yetis are said to be uncivilized humans

that actually live like apes. Although very few Sherpas claim to have actually seen a Yeti, many say that they know people who have caught glimpses of them. Some Sherpas tell of having heard the eerie, high-pitched cry of a Yeti. Many others say that they have encountered distinctive footprints in the snow. The footprints look much like those of a barefoot human, but they are wider and shorter. They have five toes, but three of them seem to have claws.

Although the Yeti is said to live only in the Himalayan Mountains, stories of the creature have spread all across the world. While the Sherpas call the beast Yeti, we probably know it best as the Abominable Snowman. And while Sherpas are convinced that the Yeti is a wild man, some Westerners have come up with different theories.

Many Westerners think that Yetis are not really human, but rather some kind of ape. Those people believe that the Yetis are the sole survivors of a type of ape that originated in China. Fossil bones prove that such apes did live in China thousands of years ago. It is possible that when the apes were dying out a few managed to climb into the Himalayas. Because those mountains are so remote and so sparsely populated, it is possible that the apes were

able to survive there for centuries with little or no contact with the rest of the world. Those who believe in this theory think that Yetis are the modern-day remnants of that group of apes.

Another Western theory is that the Yeti is the "missing link" between humans and apes. For years people have theorized that humans evolved from the apes. But no one has ever been able to find evidence of a creature that was half human, half ape. Some people believe that the Yeti is just that—the missing link between humans and lower primates.

People who believe in the existence of Yetis cannot agree on whether the creatures are ape, human, or the missing link. But all do agree on what Yetis look like. A Yeti is said to be about five feet tall, to walk on two feet, and to be covered with long, shaggy hair. That description is based on the information supplied by the mountain climbers and Sherpa guides who claim to have seen the creature. Unfortunately, no photographs of a Yeti have ever been taken. No one has ever found a Yeti's den, nor has anyone ever come across a Yeti carcass. Natives of the region have collected small scraps of bone, scalp and fur that they say come from Yetis, but there is still no absolute proof that the Yeti exists. Many skeptics think the creature is simply a product of people's imaginations.

In 1960, Sir Edmund Hillary decided to find out, once and for all, if Yetis were real. Hillary was already famous as the first person to climb Mount Everest, the tallest mountain in the world, located among the Himalayas. Hillary knew a great deal about life in the Himalayas. People thought that if anyone could find the elusive Yeti, it would be Hillary.

So the famous mountain climber put together an expedition to search for the creature. He and a group of climbers and naturalists combed the Himalayas for traces of the Yeti. But they found nothing. The best that Hillary could do was gather supposed samples of Yeti bones, scalps and skins from the Sherpas in the area.

When the samples were examined in a laboratory, scientists discovered that the Yeti remains were nothing but junk. The pointed, furry pieces of skin that the Sherpas claimed were Yeti scalps turned out to be very old goatskin caps. A microscope showed that the Yeti skins were really the skins of bears. And the Yeti bones collected by the Sherpas turned out to be bones from a variety of well-known animals such as wolves and goats.

Hillary told the world that, in his opinion, there was no such thing as a Yeti. He explained that the Sherpas are very superstitious people. They believe that their mountains are inhabited by all sorts of spirits. Hillary decided that the Yeti was simply one of those imaginary spirits. He concluded that the Sherpas saw Yetis in the mountains because they expected to see them. As Hillary pointed out, people often find exactly what they expect to find.

But if Yetis are the result of the Sherpas' imaginations, how is it that foreigners, too, have seen Yetis? One answer to that question is that Western mountain climbers really have seen creatures roaming the icy mountainsides of the Himalayas, but that the creatures were langurs, not Yetis. Langurs are monkeys that live in the mountains. They have bushy eyebrows and tufts of hair on their chins. Although langurs are smaller than Yetis are supposed to be, the two creatures do look alike. Those who don't believe in Yetis say that the descriptions of a Yeti's size are not reliable. They ask us to imagine an excited person looking at a creature running along the side of a distant mountain. It would be hard to judge just how big or small that creature really was. So, those unbelievers conclude, both Sherpas and Western climbers could easily mistake the smaller langur for the famous Yeti.

Such explanations have not, however, ended the debate over the existence of the Yeti. Sherpas argue that they could not mistake a Yeti for a langur. They note that their livelihood depends on their knowledge of the mountains and mountain animals. Many investigators agree that no one familiar with langurs could possibly mistake the monkey for an Abominable Snowman. On the other hand, no solid proof of the Yeti's existence has yet been found. So the argument continues. Until it is resolved, people will probably be eager to climb high into the Himalayan Mountains in search of a wild, hairy creature known as the Yeti. ■

If you have been timed while reading this selection, enter your reading time below. Then turn to the Words per Minute table on page 155 and look up your reading speed (words per minute). Enter your reading speed on the graph on page 156.

READING TIME: Unit 20

_____ : _____
Minutes   Seconds

How well did you read?

- *Answer the four types of questions that follow. The directions for each type of question tell you how to mark your answers.*

- *When you have finished all four exercises, check your work by using the answer key on page 152. For each right answer, put a check mark (✔) on the line beside the box. For each wrong answer, write the correct answer on the line.*

- *For scoring each exercise, follow the directions below the questions.*

A FINDING THE MAIN IDEA

Look at the three statements below. One expresses the main idea of the story you just read. A good main idea statement answers two questions: it tells *who* or *what* is the subject of the story, and it answers the understood question *does what?* or *is what?* Another statement is *too broad*, it is vague and doesn't tell much about the topic of the story. The third statement is *too narrow*, it tells about only one part of the story.

Match the statements with the three answer choices below by writing the letter of each answer in the box in front of the statement it goes with.

M—Main Idea   **B—Too Broad**   **N—Too Narrow**

_____ ☐ 1. Some people believe that hairy wild men known as Yetis live high in the Himalayas, but their existence has not been proved.

_____ ☐ 2. Some people think that there are strange, unidentified creatures living in the Himalayas.

_____ ☐ 3. Some Sherpas believe that they have found the bones, scalps and fur of Yetis.

_____ Score 15 points for a correct *M* answer

_____ Score 5 points for each correct *B* or *N* answer

_____ TOTAL SCORE: Finding the Main Idea

B RECALLING FACTS

How well do you remember the facts in the story you just read? Put an x in the box in front of the correct answer to each of the multiple-choice questions below.

1. Sherpas are
   - ___ ☐ a. wild men of the Himalayas.
   - ___ ☐ b. scientists who have found evidence of Yetis.
   - ___ ☐ c. the mountain people of the Himalayas.

2. Sir Edmund Hillary was a good person to investigate Yetis because he
   - ___ ☐ a. was an expert on wild animals.
   - ___ ☐ b. knew a lot about the Himalayas and their people.
   - ___ ☐ c. spoke the language of the Sherpas.

3. One theory about Yetis is that they are
   - ___ ☐ a. white bears.
   - ___ ☐ b. mountain goats.
   - ___ ☐ c. apes of some sort.

4. The "missing link" is a
   - ___ ☐ a. creature that connects humans to apes.
   - ___ ☐ b. type of prehistoric ape.
   - ___ ☐ c. kind of monkey that lives in the Himalayas.

5. Langurs might be what people call Yetis because they
   - ___ ☐ a. are just the size people claim Yetis to be.
   - ___ ☐ b. are hairy, with bushy eyebrows and tufts of chin hair.
   - ___ ☐ c. move quickly and try to keep away from people.

Score 5 points for each correct answer

___ TOTAL SCORE: Recalling Facts

C MAKING INFERENCES

An inference is a judgment that is made or an idea that is arrived at based on facts or on information that is given. You make an inference when you understand something that is *not* stated directly, but that is *implied*, or suggested by the facts that are given.

Below are five statements that are judgments or ideas that have been arrived at from the facts of the story. Write the letter C in the box in front of each statement that is a correct inference. Write the letter F in front of each faulty inference.

C—Correct Inference   F—Faulty Inference

- ___ ☐ 1. Hillary did not find any evidence of Yetis because he did not believe the creatures existed.
- ___ ☐ 2. Only the Sherpas believe in the existence of real wild men in the mountains.
- ___ ☐ 3. Scientists are interested in finding out exactly what the Yeti is.
- ___ ☐ 4. To the Sherpas, the Yeti is a religious figure.
- ___ ☐ 5. The Sherpas' belief that Yetis are wild men has not been changed by the arguments of Western skeptics.

Score 5 points for each correct answer

___ TOTAL SCORE: Making Inferences

D USING WORDS PRECISELY

Each of the numbered sentences below contains an underlined word or phrase from the story you have just read. Under the sentence are three definitions. One has the *same* meaning as the underlined word or phrase, one has *almost the same* meaning, and one has the *opposite* meaning. Match the definitions with the three answer choices by writing the letter that stands for each answer in the box in front of the definition it goes with.

S—Same   A—Almost the Same   O—Opposite

1. Until it is <u>resolved</u>, people will probably be eager to climb high into the Himalayan Mountains in search of the Yeti.

____ ☐ a. settled

____ ☐ b. stopped

____ ☐ c. opened to question

2. For years people have <u>theorized</u> that humans evolved from the apes.

____ ☐ a. put forward an idea

____ ☐ b. guessed

____ ☐ c. rejected an idea

3. Many <u>skeptics</u> think the creature is simply a product of people's imaginations.

____ ☐ a. believers

____ ☐ b. people who are unsure

____ ☐ c. doubters

4. People thought that if anyone could find the <u>elusive</u> Yeti, it would be Hillary.

____ ☐ a. hard to catch

____ ☐ b. easily found

____ ☐ c. secretive

5. Because those mountains are so remote and so <u>sparsely</u> populated, it is possible that the apes were able to survive there for centuries with little or no contact with the rest of the world.

____ ☐ a. hardly

____ ☐ b. thinly

____ ☐ c. heavily

____ Score 3 points for each correct *S* answer

____ Score 1 point for each correct *A* or *O* answer

____ TOTAL SCORE: Using Words Precisely

● *Enter the four total scores in the spaces below, and add them together to find your Critical Reading Score. Then record your Critical Reading Score on the graph on page 157.*

_____ Finding the Main Idea

_____ Recalling Facts

_____ Making Inferences

_____ Using Words Precisely

_____ CRITICAL READING SCORE: Unit 20

Dragons

Everyone has an idea of what dragons look like. We have seen illustrations of them. We have seen them in movies. We have read descriptions of them. Dragons are huge beasts, housetop high when they rear up. They have long, barbed tails. Smoke belches from their flaring nostrils. They exhale sheets of flame from mouths rimmed with daggerlike teeth. Their legs end in terrible long claws. Scaly armor glistens on their tough hides, and batlike wings project from their backs. Sometimes they even have more than one head! Many dragons also have the magical ability to change size at will, or to disappear.

In folktales and in fairy tales, dragons often terrorize the countryside. They swoop down from their mountain caves and incinerate villages and crops with their fiery breath. They carry away beautiful maidens and strike terror into the hearts of all but the boldest. Kings and mayors call upon brave knights or clever young princes to slay the dreadful beasts and restore peace.

Since ancient times, there have been legends of dragons. People long ago lived in fear that they might be lurking just over the horizon, out there in the next mountain range, or just over the edge of the ocean, where the earth ends. Mapmakers of long ago decorated the areas around what they believed to be a flat earth with colorful drawings of dragons. Not even the most adventuresome folk wanted to reach that point in their travels. Seamen swore that they saw steam from the breath of the beasts, far out over the billowing waves. Hunters frequently saw them circling in the air above distant peaks and saw their eyes glowing in the dark just outside the circle of campfire light.

There was no doubt in anyone's mind that dragons existed—somewhere. The Bible mentions dragons several times. The myths and folktales of ancient Britain and Europe are filled with dragons. And there was general agreement about the appearance and habits of the creatures. Even the mysterious East had dragons, although the Chinese dragons were of a more peaceful sort.

Wherever people believed in dragons, however, it's generally safe to say that the wise folk were just as happy to think that the creatures were far away, minding their own business. The more adventurous sort, of course, liked the thought that if they were lucky and brave enough, maybe they would meet and conquer a dragon and, in the process, win a fair maiden or claim the golden treasure hoard that dragons were always rumored to be hiding and guarding.

One of the best-known dragons in all of literature is the terrible Smaug in J. R. R. Tolkien's popular fantasy novel *The Hobbit*. At one point in the story, the hero, a timid little "hobbit" named Bilbo Baggins, fearfully approaches the great Smaug in his lair. Even before he sees "The Great Worm," Bilbo can hear him—a throbbing sound, "a sort of bubbling like the noise of a large pot galloping on the fire, mixed with the rumble of a giant tomcat purring." Suddenly, around a turn, there is Smaug, asleep on a vast bed of treasure.

> Smaug lay, with wings folded like an immeasurable bat, turned partly on one side, so that the hobbit could see his underparts and his long pale belly crusted with gems and fragments of gold from his long lying on his costly bed. Behind him where the walls were nearest could dimly be seen coats of mail, helms and axes, swords and spears hanging; and there in rows stood great jars and vessels filled with a wealth that could not be guessed.

In a later passage Smaug describes himself in this way:

> My armour is like tenfold shields, my teeth are swords, my claws spears, and the shock of my tail a thunderbolt, my wings a hurricane, and my breath death!

Smaug possesses many of the characteristics for which dragons have traditionally been known. But dragons are, of course, make-believe. How is it, then, that people all over the world seem to be in fairly close agreement on what they look like and how they behave?

Well, descriptions of dragons sound very much like descriptions of pterodactyls—the giant, leathery, featherless ancestors of birds. It seems to make sense that dragons would be based on the human race's memories of dinosaurs. Those giant prehistoric creatures certainly share many of the reptilian features we associate with dragons. This theory breaks down, however, when we consider that the Age of Dinosaurs ended 65 million years before there were humans on earth.

It's more likely that our ideas about dragons are based on some poor descriptions and pictures of present-day reptiles. We know that the term *dragon* is related to reptiles. It comes from the ancient Roman word *draco*, which was the name of a tree-dwelling snake said to drop from branches onto people and animals passing beneath. Those creatures swallowed their prey whole. It's probable that the draco was a giant python.

There are other ordinary creatures that

Beating its great batlike wings, the fearsome dragon rose high into the air and circled the castle. Then with a mighty rush it swooped down upon the village below and reduced the countryside for miles around to smoldering ashes with its fiery breath. Dragons are pure fantasy, of course. But if the great lizards never existed, how is it that we are all pretty much in agreement on what they look like?

also have characteristics that we associate with dragons. Crocodiles, for instance, have terrible teeth, bent legs, and thick hides. Those body parts look much like the teeth, legs, and armored hide of a dragon. People who first heard about crocodiles from someone who had seen one must have pictured a terrible creature indeed.

Even the dragon's fiery breath has a surprising parallel in the world of reptiles. The Indian cobra can spit its deadly venom as far as ten feet, blinding any victim whose eyes it reaches. It's not hard to imagine a blind traveler swearing that "the beast shot flames into my eyes and burned them out." Also, if you've ever seen a picture of a cobra drawing itself upright into position to strike, with its hood spread wide behind its frightening face, you know how easily the quick glance of a terrified person could see the wide-spread hood as wings that had lifted the creature above the ground.

Even descriptions of dragons as great flying snakes have their basis in a real creature. It is called the Draco volans. This large lizard is found in the Malay Islands. It has winglike membranes that stretch between its front and rear legs. It can leap from a limb, and by stretching its legs wide to spread the membranes, glide to another tree. It can glide for distances of up to forty feet.

You can see how such creatures grew to terrible proportions in the minds of people of long ago who were unfamiliar with them. But though in the lands of the West dragons are dreadful beasts, in the East they are usually harmless, and even good and helpful.

The dragons of China and Japan are longer and more snakelike. Modern dragon experts Paul and Karin Johsgard describe the Oriental dragon this way: "a head like a camel's, horns like a deer's, eyes like a hare's, ears like a bull's, a neck like an iguana's, a belly like a frog's, scales like a carp's, paws like a tiger's, and claws like an eagle's. The long, tendril-like whiskers extending from either side of its mouth are probably used in feeling its way along the bottom of muddy ponds. Its color varies from greenish to golden, with a series of alternating short and long spines extending down the back and along the tail, where they become longer."

Chinese historians record that there are traditionally nine types of Chinese dragons including the primitive *k'uei dragon* from which all the others evolved. The advanced species are the horned dragon, the winged dragon, the celestial dragon (which supports and protects the mansions of the gods), the spiritual dragon (which makes wind and rain), the dragon of hidden treasures (which keeps guard over concealed wealth), the coiling dragon (which lives in water), the yellow dragon (which once emerged from water and presented the legendary Emperor Fu Hsi with the elements of writing), and the dragon king, which is actually four separate creatures, each of which rules over one of the four points of the compass.

Such are the main facts about some of history's and literature's dragons. We know they don't exist, and we think we can explain how everyone came to agree on precisely what a nonexistent creature looked like. We can even understand how some people really could believe they had seen a dragon. Our imaginations are very good at assembling parts of things we *have* seen or heard about into something we *think* we have seen. There really is a rational explanation for the terrible mythical figure of the dragon. But that doesn't stop some of us from still hoping that perhaps somewhere, in a cave or on a mountain peak . . . ■

If you have been timed while reading this selection, enter your reading time below. Then turn to the Words per Minute table on page 155 and look up your reading speed (words per minute). Enter your reading speed on the graph on page 156.

READING TIME: Unit 21

_____ : _____
Minutes   *Seconds*

How well did you read?

- *Answer the four types of questions that follow. The directions for each type of question tell you how to mark your answers.*

- *When you have finished all four exercises, check your work by using the answer key on page 152. For each right answer, put a check mark (✔) on the line beside the box. For each wrong answer, write the correct answer on the line.*

- *For scoring each exercise, follow the directions below the questions.*

A FINDING THE MAIN IDEA

Look at the three statements below. One expresses the main idea of the story you just read. A good main idea statement answers two questions: it tells *who* or *what* is the subject of the story, and it answers the understood question *does what?* or *is what?* Another statement is *too broad,* it is vague and doesn't tell much about the topic of the story. The third statement is *too narrow,* it tells about only one part of the story.

Match the statements with the three answer choices below by writing the letter of each answer in the box in front of the statement it goes with.

M—Main Idea   B—Too Broad   N—Too Narrow

____ ☐ 1. Dragons have lived in myths and legends for ages, and many of their characteristics are similar to physical features and habits of some real creatures.

____ ☐ 2. Though dragons lived only in stories and in people's imaginations, the beasts seem to have some relation to reality.

____ ☐ 3. Western dragons are terrible, evil beasts, but those of the East are usually good and peaceful.

____ Score 15 points for a correct *M* answer

____ Score 5 points for each correct *B* or *N* answer

____ TOTAL SCORE: Finding the Main Idea

B RECALLING FACTS

How well do you remember the facts in the story you just read? Put an *x* in the box in front of the correct answer to each of the multiple-choice questions below.

1. Long ago, when people thought that the Earth was flat, they believed that dragons lived
   - ☐ a. in the mountains.
   - ☐ b. in caves.
   - ☐ c. just over the edges of the Earth.

2. The term *dragon* is related to
   - ☐ a. reptiles.
   - ☐ b. birds.
   - ☐ c. mammals.

3. The *draco,* which dropped from trees and swallowed their prey whole were probably
   - ☐ a. king cobras.
   - ☐ b. giant pythons.
   - ☐ c. flying lizards.

4. The hood of a cobra poised to strike may have been the basis for a dragon's
   - ☐ a. great teeth.
   - ☐ b. venom.
   - ☐ c. wings.

5. How many traditional types of Chinese dragons are there?
   - ☐ a. Nine
   - ☐ b. Thirteen
   - ☐ c. Seven

Score 5 points for each correct answer

____ TOTAL SCORE: Recalling Facts

C MAKING INFERENCES

An inference is a judgment that is made or an idea that is arrived at based on facts or on information that is given. You make an inference when you understand something that is *not* stated directly, but that is *implied*, or suggested by the facts that are given.

Below are five statements that are judgments or ideas that have been arrived at from the facts of the story. Write the letter *C* in the box in front of each statement that is a correct inference. Write the letter *F* in front of each faulty inference.

C—Correct Inference   F—Faulty Inference

____ ☐ 1. There are no evil monsters in Chinese myths and legends.

____ ☐ 2. It is likely that some types of dragons did exist around the time of the dinosaurs.

____ ☐ 3. The idea of dragons grew up from people's fears of things that they did not understand.

____ ☐ 4. Dragons stole the treasure that they guard in their lairs.

____ ☐ 5. Dragon worship was part of many ancient religious ceremonies.

Score 5 points for each correct answer

____ TOTAL SCORE: Making Inferences

D USING WORDS PRECISELY

Each of the numbered sentences below contains an underlined word or phrase from the story you have just read. Under the sentence are three definitions. One has the *same* meaning as the underlined word or phrase, one has *almost the same* meaning, and one has the *opposite* meaning. Match the definitions with the three answer choices by writing the letter that stands for each answer in the box in front of the definition it goes with.

S—Same   A—Almost the Same   O—Opposite

1. They swoop down from their mountain caves and <u>incinerate</u> villages and crops with their fiery breath.

____ ☐ a. ignite

____ ☐ b. save from destruction

____ ☐ c. burn up

2. Even the dragon's fiery breath has a surprising <u>parallel</u> in the world of reptiles.

____ ☐ a. likeness

____ ☐ b. opposite

____ ☐ c. equal

3. Chinese historians record that there are traditionally nine types of Chinese dragons, including the primitive *k'uei dragon,* from which all the others <u>evolved</u>.

____ ☐ a. died out

____ ☐ b. grew

____ ☐ c. developed

4. There really is a <u>rational</u> explanation for the terrible mythical figure of the dragon.

____ ☐ a. reasonable

____ ☐ b. senseless

____ ☐ c. likely

5. Also, if you've ever seen a picture of a cobra <u>drawing</u> itself upright into position to strike, you know how easily the quick glance of a terrified person could see the widespread hood as wings that had lifted the creature above the ground.

____ ☐ a. pulling

____ ☐ b. dragging

____ ☐ c. pushing

____ Score 3 points for each correct *S* answer

____ Score 1 point for each correct *A* or *O* answer

____ TOTAL SCORE: Using Words Precisely

● *Enter the four total scores in the spaces below, and add them together to find your Critical Reading Score. Then record your Critical Reading Score on the graph on page 157.*

____ Finding the Main Idea
____ Recalling Facts
____ Making Inferences
____ Using Words Precisely

____ CRITICAL READING SCORE: Unit 21

ANSWER KEY

1 The Cyclops

A. Finding the Main Idea
1. **M**   2. **B**   3. **N**

B. Recalling Facts
1. c   2. b   3. a   4. a   5. c

C. Making Inferences
1. **F**   2. **C**   3. **F**   4. **C**   5. **C**

D. Using Words Precisely
1. a. **S**   b. **A**   c. **O**
2. a. **A**   b. **O**   c. **S**
3. a. **A**   b. **S**   c. **O**
4. a. **O**   b. **A**   c. **S**
5. a. **S**   b. **A**   c. **O**

2 King Kong

A. Finding the Main Idea
1. **M**   2. **N**   3. **B**

B. Recalling Facts
1. c   2. b   3. b   4. b   5. a

C. Making Inferences
1. **C**   2. **F**   3. **C**   4. **F**   5. **F**

D. Using Words Precisely
1. a. **O**   b. **A**   c. **S**
2. a. **S**   b. **O**   c. **A**
3. a. **O**   b. **A**   c. **S**
4. a. **A**   b. **S**   c. **O**
5. a. **S**   b. **O**   c. **A**

3 Medusa

A. Finding the Main Idea
1. **M**   2. **N**   3. **B**

B. Recalling Facts
1. c   2. a   3. b   4. b   5. c

C. Making Inferences
1. **F**   2. **C**   3. **C**   4. **C**   5. **F**

D. Using Words Precisely
1. a. **A**   b. **S**   c. **O**
2. a. **S**   b. **O**   c. **A**
3. a. **O**   b. **A**   c. **S**
4. a. **S**   b. **A**   c. **O**
5. a. **A**   b. **S**   c. **O**

4 Bigfoot

A. Finding the Main Idea
1. **B**   2. **N**   3. **M**

B. Recalling Facts
1. b   2. c   3. b   4. b   5. c

C. Making Inferences
1. **C**   2. **C**   3. **C**   4. **F**   5. **F**

D. Using Words Precisely
1. a. **A**   b. **O**   c. **S**
2. a. **S**   b. **O**   c. **A**
3. a. **A**   b. **S**   c. **O**
4. a. **A**   b. **S**   c. **O**
5. a. **S**   b. **A**   c. **O**

5 Has Earth Been Visited by Creatures from UFOs?

A. Finding the Main Idea
1. **B**   2. **M**   3. **N**

B. Recalling Facts
1. c   2. c   3. a   4. b   5. b

C. Making Inferences
1. **F**   2. **C**   3. **C**   4. **F**   5. **F**

D. Using Words Precisely
1. a. **A**   b. **O**   c. **S**
2. a. **O**   b. **A**   c. **S**
3. a. **S**   b. **O**   c. **A**
4. a. **S**   b. **O**   c. **A**
5. a. **A**   b. **S**   c. **O**

6 The Nemean Lion and the Hound of Hell

A. Finding the Main Idea
1. **M**   2. **N**   3. **B**

B. Recalling Facts
1. b   2. a   3. b   4. c   5. a

C. Making Inferences
1. **C**   2. **F**   3. **F**   4. **C**   5. **F**

D. Using Words Precisely
1. a. **O**   b. **S**   c. **A**
2. a. **A**   b. **S**   c. **O**
3. a. **S**   b. **O**   c. **A**
4. a. **A**   b. **O**   c. **S**
5. a. **S**   b. **A**   c. **O**

7 Fabulous Fakes

A. Finding the Main Idea
1. **N**   2. **M**   3. **B**

B. Recalling Facts
1. b   2. a   3. c   4. b   5. a

C. Making Inferences
1. **C**   2. **F**   3. **C**   4. **F**   5. **F**

D. Using Words Precisely
1. a. **S**   b. **O**   c. **A**
2. a. **S**   b. **A**   c. **O**
3. a. **A**   b. **S**   c. **O**
4. a. **O**   b. **A**   c. **S**
5. a. **O**   b. **S**   c. **A**

8 Movie Monsters
A. Finding the Main Idea
1. N   2. B   3. M
B. Recalling Facts
1. b   2. c   3. a   4. b   5. c
C. Making Inferences
1. F   2. C   3. F   4. C   5. F
D. Using Words Precisely
1. a. O   b. S   c. A
2. a. S   b. O   c. A
3. a. A   b. S   c. O
4. a. A   b. O   c. S
5. a. S   b. O   c. A

9 Frankenstein's Monster
A. Finding the Main Idea
1. B   2. N   3. M
B. Recalling Facts
1. c   2. b   3. c   4. a   5. b
C. Making Inferences
1. F   2. F   3. C   4. F   5. C
D. Using Words Precisely
1. a. O   b. A   c. S
2. a. S   b. A   c. O
3. a. A   b. S   c. O
4. a. O   b. S   c. A
5. a. A   b. O   c. S

10 The Minotaur
A. Finding the Main Idea
1. N   2. B   3. M
B. Recalling Facts
1. a   2. a   3. a   4. c   5. c
C. Making Inferences
1. F   2. C   3. F   4. F   5. C
D. Using Words Precisely
1. a. S   b. O   c. A
2. a. O   b. S   c. A
3. a. A   b. O   c. S
4. a. O   b. S   c. A
5. a. S   b. A   c. O

11 Giants
A. Finding the Main Idea
1. N   2. M   3. B
B. Recalling Facts
1. b   2. a   3. c   4. c   5. c
C. Making Inferences
1. F   2. F   3. F   4. C   5. F
D. Using Words Precisely
1. a. S   b. O   c. A
2. a. S   b. A   c. O
3. a. A   b. O   c. S
4. a. S   b. O   c. A
5. a. O   b. A   c. S

12 Nessie
A. Finding the Main Idea
1. N   2. M   3. B
B. Recalling Facts
1. b   2. b   3. c   4. a   5. c
C. Making Inferences
1. F   2. C   3. F   4. C   5. F
D. Using Words Precisely
1. a. A   b. S   c. O
2. a. O   b. S   c. A
3. a. O   b. A   c. S
4. a. S   b. O   c. A
5. a. O   b. S   c. A

13 The Chimera
A. Finding the Main Idea
1. N   2. M   3. B
B. Recalling Facts
1. b   2. a   3. c   4. b   5. c
C. Making Inferences
1. F   2. C   3. F   4. C   5. F
D. Using Words Precisely
1. a. S   b. O   c. A
2. a. O   b. A   c. S
3. a. A   b. S   c. O
4. a. S   b. A   c. O
5. a. O   b. A   c. S

14 Creatures of the Imagination
A. Finding the Main Idea
1. M   2. N   3. B
B. Recalling Facts
1. b   2. a   3. c   4. b   5. c
C. Making Inferences
1. F   2. F   3. C   4. C   5. F
D. Using Words Precisely
1. a. O   b. A   c. S
2. a. S   b. O   c. A
3. a. O   b. S   c. A
4. a. O   b. A   c. S
5. a. A   b. S   c. O

15 Grendel

A. Finding the Main Idea
1. **B**   2. **N**   3. **M**

B. Recalling Facts
1. **b**   2. **c**   3. **b**   4. **a**   5. **c**

C. Making Inferences
1. **C**   2. **F**   3. **F**   4. **F**   5. **C**

D. Using Words Precisely
1. a. **A**   b. **S**   c. **O**
2. a. **O**   b. **S**   c. **A**
3. a. **S**   b. **A**   c. **O**
4. a. **S**   b. **A**   c. **O**
5. a. **A**   b. **O**   c. **S**

16 The Kraken

A. Finding the Main Idea
1. **M**   2. **N**   3. **B**

B. Recalling Facts
1. **b**   2. **c**   3. **a**   4. **b**   5. **c**

C. Making Inferences
1. **F**   2. **C**   3. **F**   4. **C**   5. **C**

D. Using Words Precisely
1. a. **S**   b. **O**   c. **A**
2. a. **A**   b. **O**   c. **S**
3. a. **A**   b. **S**   c. **O**
4. a. **A**   b. **S**   c. **O**
5. a. **S**   b. **A**   c. **O**

17 Dracula

A. Finding the Main Idea
1. **B**   2. **M**   3. **N**

B. Recalling Facts
1. **a**   2. **c**   3. **b**   4. **a**   5. **b**

C. Making Inferences
1. **F**   2. **C**   3. **F**   4. **C**   5. **F**

D. Using Words Precisely
1. a. **A**   b. **S**   c. **O**
2. a. **S**   b. **A**   c. **O**
3. a. **A**   b. **S**   c. **O**
4. a. **O**   b. **A**   c. **S**
5. a. **S**   b. **A**   c. **O**

18 The Walking Dead

A. Finding the Main Idea
1. **M**   2. **N**   3. **B**

B. Recalling Facts
1. **c**   2. **a**   3. **a**   4. **c**   5. **c**

C. Making Inferences
1. **C**   2. **F**   3. **C**   4. **F**   5. **C**

D. Using Words Precisely
1. a. **A**   b. **S**   c. **O**
2. a. **S**   b. **A**   c. **O**
3. a. **O**   b. **A**   c. **S**
4. a. **S**   b. **A**   c. **O**
5. a. **O**   b. **A**   c. **S**

19 Werewolves

A. Finding the Main Idea
1. **N**   2. **M**   3. **B**

B. Recalling Facts
1. **b**   2. **c**   3. **a**   4. **a**   5. **c**

C. Making Inferences
1. **F**   2. **F**   3. **C**   4. **F**   5. **F**

D. Using Words Precisely
1. a. **O**   b. **A**   c. **S**
2. a. **S**   b. **O**   c. **A**
3. a. **A**   b. **S**   c. **O**
4. a. **O**   b. **A**   c. **S**
5. a. **O**   b. **S**   c. **A**

20 The Yeti

A. Finding the Main Idea
1. **M**   2. **B**   3. **N**

B. Recalling Facts
1. **c**   2. **b**   3. **c**   4. **a**   5. **b**

C. Making Inferences
1. **F**   2. **F**   3. **C**   4. **F**   5. **C**

D. Using Words Precisely
1. a. **S**   b. **A**   c. **O**
2. a. **S**   b. **A**   c. **O**
3. a. **O**   b. **A**   c. **S**
4. a. **S**   b. **O**   c. **A**
5. a. **A**   b. **S**   c. **O**

21 Dragons

A. Finding the Main Idea
1. **M**   2. **B**   3. **N**

B. Recalling Facts
1. **c**   2. **a**   3. **b**   4. **c**   5. **a**

C. Making Inferences
1. **F**   2. **F**   3. **C**   4. **C**   5. **F**

D. Using Words Precisely
1. a. **A**   b. **O**   c. **S**
2. a. **S**   b. **O**   c. **A**
3. a. **O**   b. **A**   c. **S**
4. a. **S**   b. **O**   c. **A**
5. a. **S**   b. **A**   c. **O**

WORDS PER MINUTE TABLE
& PROGRESS GRAPHS

Words per Minute

Unit ▶	Sample	1	2	3	4	5	6	7	
No. of Words ▶	1027	1463	1450	981	1034	1228	1297	1209	
1:30	685	975	967	654	689	819	865	806	**90**
1:40	616	878	870	589	620	737	778	725	**100**
1:50	560	798	791	535	564	670	707	659	**110**
2:00	513	731	725	491	517	614	648	605	**120**
2:10	474	675	669	453	477	567	599	558	**130**
2:20	440	627	621	420	443	526	556	518	**140**
2:30	411	585	580	392	414	491	519	484	**150**
2:40	385	549	544	368	388	461	486	453	**160**
2:50	362	516	512	346	365	433	458	427	**170**
3:00	342	488	483	327	345	409	432	403	**180**
3:10	324	462	458	310	327	388	410	382	**190**
3:20	308	439	435	294	310	368	389	363	**200**
3:30	293	418	414	280	295	351	371	345	**210**
3:40	280	399	395	268	282	335	354	330	**220**
3:50	268	382	378	256	270	320	338	315	**230**
4:00	257	366	362	245	258	307	324	302	**240**
4:10	246	351	348	235	248	295	311	290	**250**
4:20	237	338	335	226	239	283	299	279	**260**
4:30	228	325	322	218	230	273	288	269	**270**
4:40	220	314	311	210	222	263	278	259	**280**
4:50	212	303	300	203	214	254	268	250	**290**
5:00	205	293	290	196	207	246	259	242	**300**
5:10	199	283	281	190	200	238	251	234	**310**
5:20	193	274	272	184	194	230	243	227	**320**
5:30	187	266	264	178	188	223	236	220	**330**
5:40	181	258	256	173	182	217	229	213	**340**
5:50	176	251	249	168	177	211	222	207	**350**
6:00	171	244	242	164	172	205	216	201	**360**
6:10	167	237	235	159	168	199	210	196	**370**
6:20	162	231	229	155	163	194	205	191	**380**
6:30	158	225	223	151	159	189	200	186	**390**
6:40	154	219	218	147	155	184	195	181	**400**
6:50	150	214	212	144	151	180	190	177	**410**
7:00	147	209	207	140	148	175	185	173	**420**
7:20	140	200	198	134	141	167	177	165	**440**
7:40	134	191	189	128	135	160	169	158	**460**
8:00	128	183	181	123	129	153	162	151	**480**

GROUP ONE

Minutes and Seconds ▶

◀ Seconds

GROUP TWO

Unit ▶	8	9	10	11	12	13	14	
No. of Words ▶	1453	1298	1202	1305	1283	1221	1149	
1:30	969	865	801	870	855	814	766	**90**
1:40	872	779	721	783	770	733	689	**100**
1:50	793	708	656	712	700	666	627	**110**
2:00	726	649	601	653	641	611	575	**120**
2:10	671	599	555	602	592	564	530	**130**
2:20	623	556	515	559	550	523	492	**140**
2:30	581	519	481	522	513	488	460	**150**
2:40	545	487	451	489	481	458	431	**160**
2:50	513	458	424	461	453	431	406	**170**
3:00	484	433	401	435	428	407	383	**180**
3:10	459	410	380	412	405	386	363	**190**
3:20	436	389	361	392	385	366	345	**200**
3:30	415	371	343	373	367	349	328	**210**
3:40	396	354	328	356	350	333	313	**220**
3:50	379	339	314	340	335	319	300	**230**
4:00	363	324	300	326	321	305	287	**240**
4:10	349	312	288	313	308	293	276	**250**
4:20	335	300	277	301	296	282	265	**260**
4:30	323	288	267	290	285	271	255	**270**
4:40	311	278	258	280	275	262	246	**280**
4:50	301	269	249	270	265	253	238	**290**
5:00	291	260	240	261	257	244	230	**300**
5:10	281	251	233	253	248	236	222	**310**
5:20	272	243	225	245	241	229	215	**320**
5:30	264	236	219	237	233	222	209	**330**
5:40	256	229	212	230	226	215	203	**340**
5:50	249	223	206	224	220	209	197	**350**
6:00	242	216	200	218	214	203	191	**360**
6:10	236	210	195	212	208	198	186	**370**
6:20	229	205	190	206	203	193	181	**380**
6:30	224	200	185	201	197	188	177	**390**
6:40	218	195	180	196	192	183	172	**400**
6:50	213	190	176	191	188	179	168	**410**
7:00	207	185	172	186	183	174	164	**420**
7:20	198	177	164	178	175	167	157	**440**
7:40	190	169	157	170	167	159	150	**460**
8:00	182	162	150	163	160	153	144	**480**

Minutes and Seconds ◀ / ▶ *Seconds*

GROUP THREE

Unit ▶	15	16	17	18	19	20	21	
No. of Words ▶	1228	1296	938	1093	1518	1209	1461	
1:30	819	864	625	729	1012	806	974	**90**
1:40	737	778	563	656	911	725	877	**100**
1:50	670	707	512	596	828	659	797	**110**
2:00	614	648	469	546	759	605	731	**120**
2:10	567	598	433	504	701	558	674	**130**
2:20	526	555	402	468	651	518	626	**140**
2:30	491	518	375	437	607	484	584	**150**
2:40	461	486	352	410	569	453	548	**160**
2:50	433	457	331	386	536	427	516	**170**
3:00	409	432	313	364	506	403	487	**180**
3:10	388	409	296	345	479	382	461	**190**
3:20	368	389	281	328	455	363	438	**200**
3:30	351	370	268	312	434	345	417	**210**
3:40	335	353	256	298	414	330	398	**220**
3:50	320	338	245	285	396	315	381	**230**
4:00	307	324	234	273	380	302	365	**240**
4:10	295	311	225	262	364	290	351	**250**
4:20	283	299	216	252	350	279	337	**260**
4:30	273	288	208	243	337	269	325	**270**
4:40	263	278	201	234	325	259	313	**280**
4:50	254	268	194	226	314	250	302	**290**
5:00	246	259	188	219	304	242	292	**300**
5:10	238	251	182	212	294	234	283	**310**
5:20	230	243	176	205	285	227	274	**320**
5:30	223	236	171	199	276	220	266	**330**
5:40	217	229	166	193	268	213	258	**340**
5:50	211	222	161	187	260	207	250	**350**
6:00	205	216	156	182	253	201	243	**360**
6:10	199	210	152	177	246	196	237	**370**
6:20	194	205	148	173	240	191	231	**380**
6:30	189	199	144	168	234	186	225	**390**
6:40	184	194	141	164	228	181	219	**400**
6:50	180	190	137	160	222	177	214	**410**
7:00	175	185	134	156	217	173	209	**420**
7:20	167	177	128	149	207	165	199	**440**
7:40	160	169	122	143	198	158	191	**460**
8:00	153	162	117	137	190	151	183	**480**

Minutes and Seconds ◀ / ▶ *Seconds*

Reading Speed

Directions: *Write your Words per Minute score for each unit in the box under the number of the unit. Then plot your reading speed on the graph by putting a small* **x** *on the line directly above the number of the unit, across from the number of words per minute you read. As you mark your speed for each unit, graph your progress by drawing a line to connect the* **x***'s.*

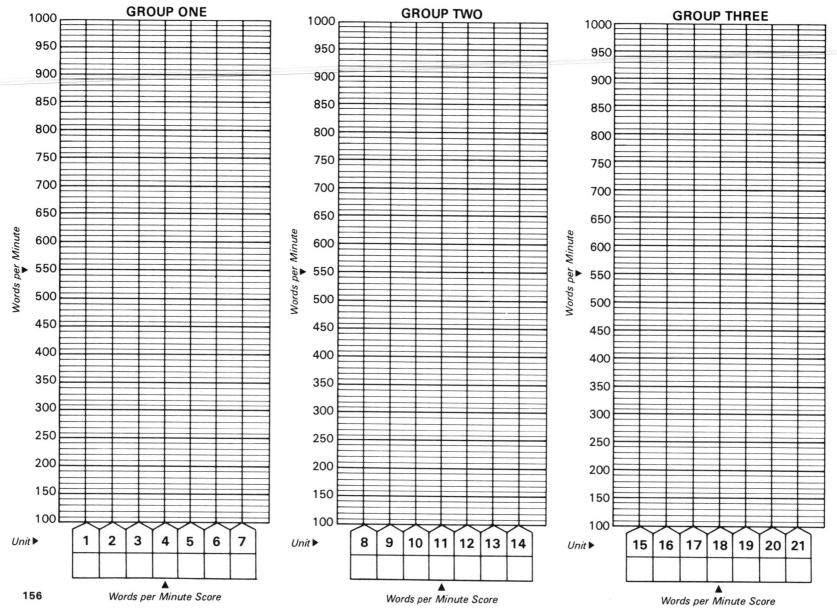

GROUP ONE

GROUP TWO

GROUP THREE

Words per Minute

Unit ▶

Words per Minute Score

156

Critical Reading Scores

Directions: *Write your Critical Reading Score for each unit in the box under the number of the unit. Then plot your score on the graph by putting a small **x** on the line directly above the number of the unit, across from the score you earned. As you mark your score for each unit, graph your progress by drawing a line to connect the **x**'s.*

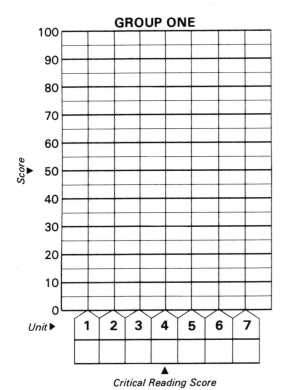

GROUP ONE

Unit ▶ | 1 | 2 | 3 | 4 | 5 | 6 | 7

Critical Reading Score

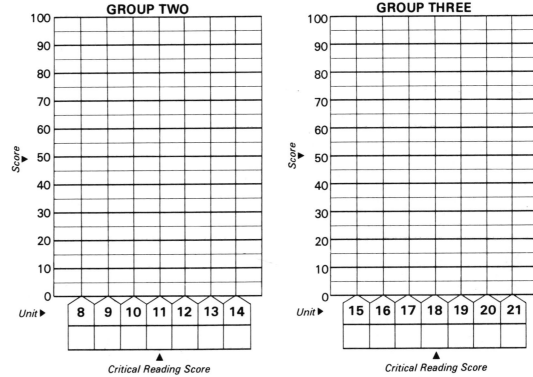

GROUP TWO

Unit ▶ | 8 | 9 | 10 | 11 | 12 | 13 | 14

Critical Reading Score

GROUP THREE

Unit ▶ | 15 | 16 | 17 | 18 | 19 | 20 | 21

Critical Reading Score

Picture Credits

Sample Unit: Movie Star News, New York

1. The Cyclops: WIDE WORLD PHOTOS

2. King Kong: Movie Star News, New York

3. Medusa: SCALA/Art Resource, New York

4. Bigfoot: © Roger Patterson, The National Audubon Society Collection/Photo Researchers, Inc.

5. Betty and Barney Hill: UPI/Bettmann Newsphotos. Alien creature: courtesy of Philip Daly

6. The Hound of Hell: The Bettmann Archive

7. Fabulous Fakes: Mermaids courtesy of Peabody Museum, Harvard University. Photograph by Hillel Burger; Cardiff Giant: New York State Historical Association

8. Movie Monsters: Jabba the Hutt © Lucasfilm Ltd. 1983. All rights reserved. Courtesy of Lucasfilm Ltd.

9. Frankenstein's Monster: Copyright © by Universal Pictures, a Division of Universal City Studios, Inc. Courtesy of MCA Publishing Rights, a Division of MCA Inc.; Mary Shelley: National Portrait Gallery, London

10. The Minotaur: Mary Evans Picture Library

11. Giants: Providence Lithograph Co. 1970

12. Nessie: BPCC/Aldus Archive

13. The Chimera: SCALA/Art Resource, New York

14. Creatures of the Imagination: John William Waterhouse's *A Mermaid* courtesy of Royal Academy of Arts, London; illustrations by Thomas Ewing Malloy

15. Grendel: Bob Eggleton

16. The Kraken: Bob Eggleton

17. Dracula: Movie Star News, New York

18. The Walking Dead: Jean-Claude Francolon/Gamma-Liaison

19. Werewolves: Copyright © by Universal Pictures, a Division of Universal City Studios, Inc. Courtesy of MCA Publishing Rights, a Division of MCA Inc. Photo courtesy of Movie Star News, New York

20. The Yeti: BPCC/Aldus Archive

21. Dragons: Bob Eggleton